EDITOR, AUTHOR, AND PUBLISHER

EDITOR
AUTHOR
AND
PUBLISHER

Papers given at the
Editorial Conference
University of Toronto, November 1968

EDITED BY Wm. J. HOWARD

Published for the Editorial Conference Committee
University of Toronto
by University of Toronto Press

Contents

Contents

Contributors

FRANCESS G. HALPENNY, managing editor of the University of Toronto Press at the time of the Conference and now general editor of the *Dictionary of Canadian Biography,* was educated at the University of Toronto. She has been involved from the earliest stages, in 1959, in the planning of the Collected Works of John Stuart Mill published by the Press and has been a member of the Editorial Committee for the project since its establishment in 1960. WELDON KEFAUVER is the director of the Ohio State University Press; ELEANOR KEWER is special projects editor at Harvard University Press; WAYLAND SCHMITT is humanities editor, Yale University Press; R. J. SCHOECK, professor of English, University of Toronto, is editing one of the volumes in the Yale Edition of St. Thomas More.

PHILIP KOLB, professor of French, University of Illinois, was educated at the University of Chicago, the Sorbonne, and Harvard. His chronology and critical commentary on Proust's published correspondence was awarded a prize by the Académie française in 1951. In 1952 he was commissioned by Proust's heirs and publishers to prepare a critical, fully annotated edition of all the author's available correspondence. Several volumes of these letters, as well as various studies of the Proust's works, have appeared. Professor Kolb has in preparation a biographical study based in part on unpublished sources of material.

A. WALTON LITZ, associate professor of English, Princeton University, was educated at Princeton and the University of Oxford. He is the author of *The Art of James Joyce* (1951), *Jane Austen: A Study of Her Artistic Development* (1965). He has edited *Modern American Fiction: Essays in Criticism* (1963) and annotated editions of *Pride and Prejudice, Return of the Native*, and *Dubliners*. His major interests are criticisms of prose fiction and modern poetry, and he is currently at work on a critical study of Wallace Stevens.

SIMON NOWELL-SMITH, formerly librarian of the London Library, president of the (London) Bibliographical Society, and Lyell Reader in Bibliography in the University of Oxford, was educated at Sherborne and New College, Oxford. His publications include *The Legend of the Master* (Henry James) (1946), *Browning, Poetry and Prose* (edited) (1950), *The House of Cassell* (1958), *Letters to Macmillan* (1967), *International Copyright Law and the Publisher in the Reign of Queen Victoria* (1968).

GEORGE L. PARKER, assistant professor of English at the Royal Military College, Kingston, was educated at Mount Allison University and Pennsylvania State University. He taught for some years at Regina College in the University of Saskatchewan. He received his PH.D. at the University of Toronto in 1969. The subject of his paper is drawn from his dissertation on the relations between publishing and the profession of writing in Canada from 1890 to 1940.

EDITOR, AUTHOR, AND PUBLISHER

Introduction

Wm. J. HOWARD

For the origin of Books, we have nothing that is clear: the books
of Moses are doubtless the oldest of all that are extant; but there
were books before those of Moses, who cites several; Scipio
Sgambati, and others even talk of books before the deluge, written
by the patriarchs Adam, Seth, Enos, Cainan ... Noah and his wife,
also by Ham, and Japhet and his wife; besides others by dæmons
or angels; of all which some moderns have found enough to fill an
antediluvian library ...

When Ephraim Chambers wrote this section for his entry
under "book" in the 1738 edition of his *Cyclopaedia*, he did not
accept the history he was presenting, he merely recorded it. I
should like to use him as a model in introducing this work and
say that once upon a time, many many years ago, so a seven-
teenth-century pamphlet relates, a gentleman by the name of
Faustus bargained with a friend about something or other,
thereby introducing printing into Europe, and beginning a long-
lasting relationship – that between author, editor, and publisher,
for the Faustus legend was subsequently disproved through the

efforts of patient and judicious scholarship. But rumour has it that the legend is not completely without foundation; bedeviling problems have plagued the relationship ever since. Witness the problems between Dryden and Tonson, Swift and Motte, or Fielding and Millar. But once again patient and judicious scholarship clarified the bedevilment. Dryden and Tonson had a personality clash; Swift made no comment on the publication of the *Travels* until after the work appeared; and if Millar purchased *Tom Jones* sight unseen, he caused his own problems, as any editor will tell you. On the other hand Richardson's relations with his publisher were harmonious; he published his own works. All publishing relationships have not been that single-handed. At another point in his entry under "book" Chambers evaluates the work of one particular author in these words:

He sets out with a tedious preamble, perhaps foreign to the question; and proceeds on to a digression, which gives rise to a second; which carries him such length that we lose sight of him: he oppresses us with proofs of things that needed none; makes objections no body would have thought of, and to answer them is sometimes forced to make a dissertation ...

Anyone today would say that the author in question needed a firm editor. And so the fourth Editorial Problems Conference, held at St. Michael's College in the University of Toronto, 8 and 9 November 1968, desired to explore the relationship between authors, editors, and publishers.* Their plans became a reality through a generous grant from the Canada Council, and the gracious co-operation of interested scholars from Canada, Britain, and the United States. Wisely, however, the conference did not begin with the Faustus legend or even with Chambers; its limits were much more modest.

*Members of the Committee for the 1968 conference were G. E. Bentley, Jr., David Esplin, Francess Halpenny, Wm. J. Howard, J. A. McClelland, J. M. Robson, R. J. Schoeck, and D. I. B. Smith.

The conference began realistically with a reception and a cocktail party sponsored by the University of Toronto Press and was followed by a dinner at which Mr. M. Jeanneret, director of the University of Toronto Press, welcomed the delegates. After dinner, Mr. Simon Nowell-Smith gave the introductory address, a light-hearted historical survey of the norms and prejudices of late nineteenth-century editors toward their authors and reading public; this setting had the very happy function of locating editors and editorial policies within a context in which much larger questions might be explored. The author queried the practices of twentieth-century editors, not for the purpose merely of challenging them, but in order to provide a forum for discussing the contemporary assumptions and procedures of scholars and academic presses. Mr. Nowell-Smith concluded by proposing several norms of his own as possible guides. Throughout the conference, the questions Mr. Nowell-Smith raised were discussed again and again.

On Saturday morning Mr. George Parker examined the history of Canadian publishing during the early decades of the present century and demonstrated the importance of copyright laws in the development of Canadian publishing. Mr. Parker also indicated source material for further investigation and outlined problems in Canadian publishing that have yet to be explored. The student of Canadian publishing will find Mr. Parker's paper both informative and challenging.

The second morning session was devoted to the practical considerations involved in publishing; it was composed of a panel of experts in practical publishing from four university presses involved in the production of multi-volume editions. Miss Francess Halpenny described the very realistic and necessary general planning that is involved in any successful large-scale editorial project. After distinguishing between various types of editions she suggested some guidelines which might be of benefit to critics reviewing these editorial projects. Mr.

Wayland Schmitt, drawing on his experience of editing large projects at Yale, developed reasons for close co-operation between scholars and editors from the beginning of a project. Mr. Weldon A. Kefauver concentrated on distinguishing between the purposes for different types of editions, and Mrs. Eleanor Kewer, in a most enjoyable talk, presented several very practical solutions to problems involved in the physical presentation of large editions. Rounding out the session, Professor R. J. Schoeck gave a brief clarification of the distinctly different types of group projects. The members of the conference received the very valuable impressions that they had been eavesdropping on a working session of editors and had become richer for the experience. I would hope that the papers as published here still retain some of that flavour.

After moving from general norms through the practical considerations of editing, the afternoon sessions explored two examples of the important role the editor has played in publishing literary as opposed to scholarly works. Addressing himself to the life of Proust, Professor Philip Kolb described Proust's changing attitudes towards publishers; at first antipathetic to and inept in his relations with them, his relationship with one editor altered the course of his subsequent career and helped to complete one of the most important works of twentieth-century French literature. Drawing on new material from the Scribner archives at Princeton University, Professor A. Walton Litz not only described the way Maxwell Perkins changed the image of Scribners, bringing their publishing policy into the twentieth century; he also presented a picture of a sensitive editorial talent that could both appreciate the spirit of an author's emerging work and aid in its final production. Using new and extremely interesting material about Fitzgerald, Hemingway, and Wolfe, Professor Litz left no doubt of the importance of Maxwell Perkin's role as a critical and therefore, perhaps, "creative" editor of literature.

The papers from the fourth Editorial Problems Conference

then are a record of several facets of a contemporary editorial relationship and, it is hoped, will present a useful and informative book – the purpose of every author, editor, and publisher. As Chambers wrote in 1738:

The uses of books are numerous: they make one of the chief instruments, or means of acquiring knowledge; they are the repositories of laws, and the vehicles of learning of every kind: our religion itself is founded on books: without them, says Bartholin, God is silent, justice dormant, physic at a stand, philosophy lame, letters dumb, and all things involved in Cimmerian darkness.

Overstated perhaps but a consolation nonetheless to those interested in the contents of this volume and the problems to which it addresses itself.

Authors, Editors, and Publishers

SIMON NOWELL-SMITH

IN 1843 THE LONDON PUBLISHER John Murray told Sir Francis Head, lately lieutenant governor of Upper Canada, at Government House, Toronto, that the democratic tendency of native American publications was sapping the principles and loyalty of colonial subjects of the Queen. Publishers in pursuit of their commercial aims will use any argument, catch at any straw. Murray saw cheap United States books entering the northern provinces and underselling the editions in which he held the British copyrights. His pocket was hit, and in its defence he wrote of patriotism to the colonial administrator, and of the national economy to Mr. Gladstone, president of the Board of Trade.

To potential customers he addressed yet another argument. Settlers in the backwoods of North America, he said, had probably never dreamed that in buying foreign piracies they were doing an injustice to authors "for whose works they perhaps entertain the sincerest devotion." There was no conscious hypocrisy in this. None of the succession of John Murrays since the eighteenth century has been a hypocrite. All were good friends to their authors: even the burning of Byron's memoirs

in the fireplace of John Murray II, a fireplace that still illumines
the colloquies of John Murray VI and Byron scholars, was an act
of honest, if misguided, friendship.

But in the minds of publishers there is, and always has been,
something of a dichotomy. I occasionally wonder whether
schizophrenia is not their occupational hazard, or even perhaps
a prerequisite of success. On the one hand, when challenged,
they justify their profits, and their reluctance to publish meritorious works with no hope of profit, by insisting that (as one of
them put it in the 1930s) they "are ordinary commercial men,
and their purposes are ordinary commercial purposes." I could
cap this quotation from almost every decade of the last two
hundred years. On the other hand, as was once said by Mr.
Harold Macmillan, a publisher both before and since his term
as British prime minister, "Our guiding principle is that publishers exist to satisfy their authors."

Publishers best satisfy their authors by selling their books.
Authors are dissatisfied when they think the publishers are not
doing everything possible, by display and advertisement, to sell
their books. This is no less true of best-selling authors than of
those whose books sell not at all. My quotation from Mr.
Macmillan comes from a letter to the best-selling Hugh Walpole,
whose obsessive concern with publicity more than once moved
Macmillan's to increase his allotment of advertising space –
which they did simply as an act of grace: like many other
publishers Macmillan's put less faith in advertising than authors
commonly do. Rudyard Kipling was similarly obsessed. When
his secretary, visiting a relative in a dockyard town in the first
world war, reported that there were no copies of *Fringes of the
Fleet* on the bookstalls, Kipling, writing through his agent, so
castigated Macmillan's that they were goaded into replying – to
the agent – "If Mr. Kipling will send out spies ..."

I have nothing to say, or at least I am going to say nothing on
this occasion, against literary agents. But the markedly different relations between Kipling and Macmillan's, and between
Walpole and Macmillan's, does illustrate one point I want to

make. Kipling had almost no direct contact, either personally or in correspondence, with his publishers: Walpole was in frequent communication with the same publishers, and looked to them, not only for encouragement and friendship, but to edit his manuscripts and set him right when he confused the names or ages of his characters, or the colour of their eyes, or forgot whether they were childless or had families. Friendship and editorship play a part in satisfying authors. It is about these, rather than about the commercial aspects of publishing or the loyalty of her Canadian subjects to the Queen, that I propose to talk this evening. I shall deal first with the relationship between author and publisher-as-editor, chiefly in the nineteenth century, and then say something about the relationship that exists in the twentieth century between the academic editor of nineteenth-century letters and the academic publisher.

What responsibility has a publisher, what responsibility ought a publisher to have, as editor of writings he is about to present to the public in print – perhaps the writings of a budding genius whose every quirk of spelling and punctuation will come under the magnifying glass of the textual critic of a later age? Faced with an unknown writer he may have a hunch, but he can have no certainty, that the man is a genius, or will be judged so by posterity. An obscure young poet called Keats? or Yeats? Are his punctuation, even his versification, to be "improved"? Or young Algernon Swinburne, with the beginnings of fame and a good chance of good sales? Is the "fleshliness" of his verses to be modified? Keats's first publisher was glad to be shot of him almost before his first book was published: so was the first publisher of the first of Swinburne's books to achieve notoriety.

   The experiences of these two poets were somewhat different. Swinburne was incensed against Moxon because of innumerable errors in *Poems and Ballads* (1866) – involving a couple of dozen cancels – though whether the errors were not partly the result of the author's carelessness in manuscript or in correcting proof history does not relate. Keats, after his *Poems* (1817) was transferred from the Olliers to Taylor and Hessey, grew to rely greatly on the friendship, criticism, and editorship of John Taylor. One of his debts of gratitude was for the trouble Taylor took over the manuscript of *Endymion* (1818). "I will attend to the punctuations you speak of," Keats wrote. "The comma should be at *soberly*, and in the other passage the comma should follow *quiet*. I am extremely indebted to you for this attention and also for your after admonitions." And again, "The preface is well without those things you have left out." Not every young poet submits to his publisher's admonitions, allowing him to tamper with commas, or with a preface already once rewritten at the admonition of another friend. It is true that a year or two later Taylor over-reached himself, tampering with the text of *The Eve of St. Agnes.* "My meaning is quite destroyed in the alteration," wrote Keats.

The moral, perhaps, is that commas are in the publisher's legitimate field, but that destroying meaning is not. It is on record that Yeats trusted his publishers to attend to his "idiosyncratic and unreliable" punctuation. (One cannot imagine the same to be true of E. E. Cummings or Ezra Pound, nor – in prose – of that most idiosyncratic of punctuators, Charles Dickens.) In one respect I think it will be agreed that a publisher has a duty to his author. Many years ago I asked a friend who had published a lecture by Professor Lord David Cecil why, misquotations apart, he had allowed the professor consistently to split *Redgauntlet* into two words – *Red Gauntlet*. The reply was, "We should never think of doubting a distinguished scholar." This from a publisher who was also the most distinguished bibliographer of nineteenth-century fiction of his day.

Where the publisher-as-editor is most likely to come into conflict with his author is in the field of censorship. No author has ever relished censorship, public or private. He may appreciate that it is not only he, but the publisher, printer, bookseller, and librarian who are liable to pay the penalty for disseminating matter that judge or jury will deem offensive to the law. But many authors do not accept that the publisher has as good a right to reject, or ask for modifications in, a book on the personal ground that he dislikes the author's subject or his opinions or his mode of expression, or on the commercial ground that the public will dislike them, as on the precautionary ground that the law may condemn them.

I have chosen a few examples of unofficial censorship in and after the Victorian period to illustrate various points:

(a) that the publisher may have personal scruples;

(b) that he will not wish to alienate the particular public or "constituency" on whose continued goodwill his business depends;

(c) that publishers who accept books they have not read are asking for trouble; and

(d) that authors who resent interference tend to rationalize their resentment by taking a high moral line about literary integrity in conflict with their publishers' more conventional, or prudential, views of public morality or religion.

John Murray III entered into an agreement with Harriet Martineau for a book, as yet unwritten, about her travels in Egypt. In *Eastern Life, Past and Present* (1848), when the first part of the manuscript reached him, Murray detected several "flings at Religion": there was the insinuation that Moses had been no more divinely aided than Plato, and the attempt to prove that the human race was of much greater antiquity than could be deduced from the Old Testament. Murray wrote to the author that he could not publish this "work of infidel tendency" with its "obvious aim of deprecating the authority and invalidating the veracity of the Bible." To which Miss Martineau replied that she had without difficulty found another publisher. "Otherwise I should have taken steps to compel you to fulfil your engagement ... I have, therefore, only to regret your presumptuous and immature decision on the character of the work, and your mistake in beginning the negotiation as a

man of business and breaking it off as a Censor of the Press."
(The same John Murray, incidentally, was later to publish
Darwin's *On the Origin of Species* and *The Descent of Man.*)

Murray's attitude was paralleled seventy years later by George
H. Doran of New York. A sincere Evangelical who was yet
liberal enough to publish for a Roman Catholic priest and a
Jewish rabbi, Doran drew the line at a novel in which one of his
successful authors advocated sex outside wedlock. "I would
publish no book which destroyed a man's simple faith in God
without providing an adequate substitute. I would publish no
book which would destroy the institution of marriage without
providing a substitute order of society which would be protec-
tive of the younger generations. All else I would cheerfully
publish." Doran called this his "publishing *credo*": the author,
Cosmo Hamilton, called it "a confession of sheer cowardice."

Editors of Victorian magazines, who in this context may be
lined up with the publishers their employers, went in constant
fear of Mrs. Grundy or, as one of them put it, of "that blatant
beast, the public." Not all of them rose to the flight of Thackeray
when rejecting a poem sent by Mrs. Browning to the *Cornhill*
in 1861: "You see that our magazine is written not only for men
and women, but for boys, girls, infants, sucklings almost, and
one of the best wives, mothers, women in the world writes some
verses which I feel certain would be objected to by many of our
readers ... In your poem, you know, there is an account of
unlawful passion felt by a man for a woman." Mrs. Browning
replied: "I confess it, dear Mr. Thackeray, never was anyone
turned out of a room for indecent behaviour in a more gracious
and conciliatory manner! ... But I am deeply convinced that the
corruption of our society requires, not shut doors and windows,
but light and air."

A few months earlier Thackeray had rejected a story in which
Anthony Trollope had introduced not only unlawful passion
but illegitimate children. Trollope replied with bantering allu-
sions to similar "naughtinesses" in Scott's, George Eliot's, and

Thackeray's own novels, as well as to that "very fie-fie story," *Oliver Twist*. But he took Thackeray's point: "An impartial editor must do his duty. Pure novels must be supplied. And the owner of the responsible name [that is, the publisher of the *Cornhill*] must be the judge of the purity ... A man who allows himself to be irritated because judgment goes against himself is an ass." As a novelist Thackeray himself wrote with the consciousness of Mrs. Grundy looking over his shoulder, but he had his own subtle methods of hoodwinking her.

Another headache was engendered in the editors by serialization. They would print the early instalments of a novel without knowing how the story was to turn out. The editor of *Macmillan's Magazine* could not foresee that a third of the way through *Old Sir Douglas* (1886–87) Caroline Norton would slip in a chapter derogatory of Queen Victoria and her court: the serial was suspended for three months while the author first threatened to withhold the rest altogether and later modified the offending passages – in spite of her conviction that "the groundwork of the story, the characters in the story, and the opinions advanced in it, are (as I have said) *warp and woof*, and not beads strung on a thread to be pulled off at pleasure." The editor of *Cassell's Magazine*, with its reputation for wholesome "family reading" for the lower middle class, could not know that in *A Terrible Temptation* (1871) Charles Reade intended, as he confided to his diary, "to tell the truth soberly, *viz.*, that young men of fortune have all mistresses; and that these are not romantic creatures, but only low, uneducated women bedizened in fashionable clothes." Nor could Cassell's know, when they blue-pencilled a "Damn it" in Wilkie Collins's *Man and Wife* (1869–70), that he would treat them to a homily.

Readers who object to expletives in books are – as to my experience – readers who object to a great many other things in books, which they are too stupid to undersand. It is quite possible that your peculiar constituency may take exception to things to come in my story, which are essential to the development of character, or which are connected with a much higher and larger moral point of view than they are capable of taking themselves. In these cases I am afraid you will find me deaf to all remonstrances – in those best interests of the independence of literature which are *your* interests (properly understood) as well as mine.

Reade, smarting under censorship of his "strong and true dialogue and situations," told Cassell's that "whatever I write and sign with my name will be commented on as mine, and nobody will ever dream of blaming an editor or publisher." Few editors or publishers would agree to this. As Macmillan's editor told Mrs. Norton, "We, as connected with *Macmillan's Magazine*, should be culpable, and should be held culpable, if, in whatever circumstances and under whatever name, that chapter appeared in its pages."

Forty years later a Macmillan of the next generation rejected H. G. Wells's *Ann Veronica* (1909) as "exceedingly distasteful to the public which buys books published by our firm," and forty years later again the same firm used almost the same words when insisting that Sean O'Casey moderate his colourful profanities. Meanwhile, within eighteen months of their shocked rejection of *Ann Veronica*, the firm provided a classic example of the foolhardiness of not only contracting for a book and paying an advance on it, but sending it to the printer, unread. They had understood that *The New Machiavelli* (1911) was to be a political novel, but it turned out to deal with "social questions, and particularly with the question of sex." "Every novel," Wells replied, "*must* have a sexual interest. I quite perceive, however, that there are strong practical objections to forcing a publisher who has changed his mind about a book to go on with its publication ... I don't want litigation if it can possibly be helped." There was no litigation, but Macmillan's, with the threat over their heads and the printer's bill in their hands, appealed to five other publishers before they found the baby a good home.

As at last example of an author's attitude to the publisher *qua* censor, Richard Aldington once wrote to Alec Craig, author of *The Banned Books of England* (1962),

Each of my novels has been more or less mutilated in the interests of prudery by my English publishers. I don't in the least blame them, they are only doing what I should do in their position, i.e. trying to guard themselves against the working of a law which is vaguely worded and capriciously administered ... I shall henceforth issue the complete text of my books in America, and with indifference allow the English to make what cuts their absurd prejudices demand.

Mr. Craig, a strong advocate of freedom of expression by serious writers, supports unofficial censorship when he argues that legal responsibility should rest on the publisher, who is "in a far better position than the author to judge the climate of public taste and legal opinion."

Censorship, of course, is only one of the cares of the publisher-as-editor. However I do not propose to go more deeply into the censorious functions fulfilled today by the publisher's bodyguard of specialist "readers" outside the firm, trained "readers" inside the firm, legal advisers, copy-editors. I have said enough – and I hope said it soberly enough – about ancient history. Now I want to deal, more provocatively, with a specific twentieth-century problem, the editing by scholars for publication of the letters of authors – by which I mean the correspondence of men of letters – of the nineteenth century. The relevance of what has gone before to what is now to come will, I hope, eventually become clear.

The problem of how letters should be presented to the reader has exercised many minds. It is a subject on which my own views may be thought too intemperate for full expression in the present urbane company. Moreover it is only relevant this evening insofar as a publisher has any justification in seeking to influence the editorial methods of a scholar. I think the publisher has some justification, and even a duty: and when I say a publisher I mean of course a publisher of good academic standing – say, a major university press with a reputation to sustain.

Every scholarly editor will have his own views on how to present his material, and different materials may demand different treatment. But should the scholar demand absolute autonomy? I am going to advocate a degree of self-denial on the part of editors, on the ground that absolute autonomy corrupts absolutely.

The basic question is, For whom are the letters of famous authors collected, edited, and published? In the nineteenth century the answer would have been, For an educated public among whom only a small minority are academic specialists. Today the answer is that all too often the only user – I do not say reader – the editor seems to have in mind is a specialist like himself. Few cultured readers outside the Eng. Lit. sector of the Ed. Biz. can read, with concentration and pleasure, pages uglified by all the typographical devices and obtrusions of a modern edited text – the brackets of various shapes and sizes; the solidi and the single or double vertical rules; the typographical underlining or double underlining of what would conventionally be printed in italics or small caps; the scored-through deletions and superscript second thoughts that break up the printed page with wide-open white spaces; the ampersands of capital-letter dimensions that stare out from the page to represent the modest plus-sign of the rapid letter-writer; and the overworked and often misused "*sic*": all the devices, in fact, that may be appropriate to the understanding of a poet writing poetry (say Keats writing *Hyperion*), but that are, in my view, inappropriate to a poet writing to his fiancé or his solicitor or his publisher.

What end do all these editorial devices serve? I am reminded of De Quincey's distinction between *Literae humaniores* (that is, Literature) and *Literae didacticae* (what De Quincey called Anti-literature). *Literae didacticae* means "teaching-books." I believe that much modern research and criticism and editing is antipathetic to literature: it is the enemy of true literature, an enemy unavowed and the more dangerous for being so, for not being recognized by the practitioners of Eng. Lit. as inimical to what should be their own proper purposes.

The editor of Keats's letters quotes with approbation Mr. W. H. Auden's prophecy that one day those letters may be more widely read and admired than Keats's poetry itself. Not, I fear, more widely read in Professor Rollins's edition. The wider reading public does not take kindly to a proliferation of brackets and "braces." Even the academic student of *Hyperion*, with all its manuscript revisions, is not helped, when reading Keats's letters as background to his studies, or reading them perhaps for pure pleasure, by editorial obtrusions. "I have also been writing parts of my Hyperion," wrote Keats to Benjamin Bailey. The original letter is torn or indistinct. "I {hav}e a{l}so been writing parts of my Hyperion," prints Professor Rollins.

Before I bring the publisher back into my argument – the argument being that the publisher should share the responsibility for the editorial techniques – I want to give specific examples of what, in my personal view, has gone wrong with the editing of letters. There is good reason, I concede, for the minute examination of manuscripts of creative literature and for recording all variants in a "teaching-book" – provided, that is, that the non-specialist educated public is given also a considered text in which the poet can be read as literature. There is no justification, I maintain, for adopting the full "teaching-book" prescription for letters – the more so because "teaching-books" of letters are rarely followed by editions for general readers. When in a letter Keats, *currente calamo*, writes "though" for "thought," why enclose the final *t* in square brackets? When the *o* in "not" has disappeared through wear and tear of the paper, may not the editor supply it tacitly, without benefit of "curly braces"? I mentioned earlier Keats's gratitude to John Taylor for attending to his punctuation. Maybe Keats would not have relished the idea of his letters to Fanny Brawne being published at all: quite certainly he would not have felt grateful to an editor who regarded a misplaced and cancelled comma as "a reading of interest or significance," worthy of immortality entombed between angle-brackets.

In matters of punctuation and spelling the Victorians had a code of good manners. (I am not speaking about their editorial misdemeanours, as we now count them, in other respects.) Dickens's sister-in-law and daughter would no more have allowed Dickens to misspell "phenomenon" in a published letter, as his modern editors do, than would the printer, or John Forster as proof-reader, have let the misspelling slip through in one of Dickens's novels. Anthony Trollope's son, preparing his father's posthumous *Autobiography*, corrected his father's habitual misspelling of George Eliot with a double *l* and a double *t*: what is there to be gained by perpetuating the error as the modern editor of Trollope's letters does? (No one could call Trollope's letters creative literature.) If consistent misspellings, or the slightest slip of the letter-writer's pen, the *ipsissimi lapsus calami*, are deemed, perhaps for some psychological reason, to be significant, need they be pinpointed in the text rather than relegated to an *apparatus criticus* or to the editor's justificatory introduction?

And there is another point. If you read Shelley's letters you will find a series addressed to Thomas Jefferson Hogg at the time when both were flirting with the Westbrook sisters: Shelley, you will remember, was to marry one of them, and Hogg, subsequently, to make love to her. Fairly far on in the correspondence Shelley asks Hogg, "Pray, which of the Miss W's do *you* like?" If this is not hearing Shelley plain, I do not know what is. Rossetti, in a letter about the Brownings, refers to "Mrs. B": disrespectful, perhaps, but can you doubt that Rossetti would have spoken so of her? Yet their editors must print "the Miss W[estbrook]s" and "Mrs. B[rowning]." No doubt the day will come when we shall not be allowed to read *"Dear Mrs. B. – Chops and tomato-sauce. Yours, Pickwick."* Of these editorial incongruities – the Miss W's and Mrs. B – I would only say that it is a pity they did not catch the eye of a publisher's reader or editor, someone whose detachment from the actual grind of textual editing would have led him to feel that communication between Shelley or Rossetti and the educated reading public mattered more than communication between the textual editor and that public. (The textual editors just quoted, incidentally, either had no ears to hear, or else they reckoned that their readers were morons.)

But more important than this is the wider question of the degree to which the editor should be free to indulge his own preferences, and the degree to which the publisher should be allowed to control him. I have spoken of the Victorian code of good editorial manners. What I should like to see is a publisher's code of guidance to editors. I am not suggesting a fixed set of rules, but recommendations from which editors would only be expected to depart if they could show good reason.

You may ask, Why a publisher's code and not a code hammered out by a committee of scholarly editors? I think there should perhaps be both. It will be a happy day when scholarly editors, concerned with manuscripts of poetry and other works of creative literature, agree among themselves about what should be understood by various shapes of brackets. They don't yet agree. Many editors in recent years have used angle brackets for authors' deletions and braces for *lacunae*: others have quite precisely reversed this usage.

But the standardization of such devices in the edited text of a work of creative literature is a very different thing from a set of standards for presenting the letters of an author, or of any other man, to an educated public. It is here that, I think, the publisher should have his say. My code of guidance would adopt the standards of the committee of scholarly editors in such matters as brackets, if diversity of brackets were deemed, in a particular instance, to be necessary. The code would also cover such

matters as spelling, capitalization, punctuation, the expansion
of abbreviations, even paragraphing. (It is a relief to find the
editors of Mrs. Gaskell's letters writing, "Intolerably long paragraphs have been broken down." There's one for the code.) The
dashes of every kind of length that Sydney Smith used for punctuation; the two dots which in Browning's autograph are often
indistinguishable from comma-dash or period-dash; George
Eliot indifferently underlining the titles of her books, or putting
them in double quotes or single quotes or no quotes at all; again,
Sydney Smith's habit of omitting the *e* in past participles without inserting an apostrophe (of which his editor remarks, "This
idiosyncrasy, I felt, would become irritating in a printed text");
the contracted forms of words like "which" and "would" that
some editors expand and others prefer to retain; the "Mr" with
an elevated "r", with or without period, and the "&c" with
ampersand and elevated "c" ... these would all be subject to the
discipline of something analogous to a publisher's normal house
style. So would the placing of address and date at the head of a
letter, wherever the writer might have placed them, and the
degree of indentation of openings and closings like "My dear
Haydon" and "Yours eternally, John Keats." (In one edition
of some of the Rossettis' letters the editor is faithful not only to
the writers' whims in indenting the opening salutation, but also
to their use or non-use of a comma at the end of it.) When
George Eliot writes two letters on one day, one with her address
engraved and the other with the identical address in manuscript,
Professor Haight uses different types to distinguish them. Is this
important? I don't know – I'm asking you. I should have
thought that if there was any significance the editor would have
explained it. But he doesn't.

Of course absolute uniformity of practice is not desirable.
Professor Earl Griggs would have little difficulty in justifying
his retention of Coleridge's unorthodox spellings and capricious
use of capitals; and Sir Rupert Hart-Davis could equally justify

his rejection of Oscar Wilde's eccentricities of the same nature. In the one instance the eccentricities are part of the flavour of the letters, in the other not: Wilde used capitals arbitrarily to serve the purpose of calligraphy, not of sense, and the effect is not reproducible in type.

But the fact that absolute uniformity is undesirable need not prevent the publisher from laying down general principles, for example, that obvious slips of the pen should be silently corrected. In the introduction to his *Letters of Coleridge* Professor Griggs writes, "Obvious slips of the pen, such as the repetition of a word, have been silently corrected." Wilde's editor and many others have said much the same. They would not have perpetuated Rossetti's "would of course have been duly duly [*sic*] felt."

But here I must insert a footnote. I quoted Professor Griggs as having written, "Obvious slips of the pen ... have been silently corrected." As printed, however, the sentence reads, "Obviously slips of the pen ... have been silently corrected," which is not what the professor, the least didactic of men, consciously intended. I ought to have quoted "Obviously [*sic*] ..." to indicate my awareness of the subconscious working of Professor Griggs's mind. And I endorse what I interpert to have been his subconscious thought: "Obviously slips of the pen, such as the repetition of a word, *ought* to be silently corrected." Another for the code.

I cannot, however, in Toronto, overlook that other great Coleridge scholar, Professor Kathleen Coburn. Of Coleridge's *Notebooks* she writes, "Slips of the pen are to be respected," and she quotes Coleridge himself in support. A hundred years in advance of his time, Coleridge held the almost Freudian view that "It is worth noting, and endeavouring to detect, the Law of the Mind by which, in writing earnestly while we are thinking, we omit words necessary to the sense." But Professor Coburn was editing Coleridge's *Notebooks*. She went on to draw a distinction between, on the one hand, "casual, private, uncorrected and uncompleted" manuscript notebooks, which demand *"literatim* transcription," and, on the other hand, "poems, or even letters, where the writer's intention to communicate gives an editor clearer directives." Communication is the nub of the matter. The editor's task is to facilitate the same communication between letter-writer and modern reader as the letter-writer was seeking to establish between himself and his correspondent.

Editing Clough's correspondence Professor Frederick Mulhauser made one of my points for me. In order that his printed text should be "readable as well as accurate" he made "no attempt ... to reproduce the appearance of the manuscript. Clough had no unusual or amusing idiosyncrasies in writing a letter, and the personality of his letters does not grow out of the appearance of the manuscript." Here is raw material for another recipe in the publisher's cook book. Unless it can be persuasively argued that a writer's idiosyncrasies are integral to the personality of his letters, then his idiosyncrasies, as well as his inconsistencies and slips of the pen, should be ironed out by the editor. Coleridge, perhaps, on one side of the line; Clough and the Rossettis, Trollope and Oscar Wilde on the other; and no doubt many borderline cases. And to my mind the publisher, whose interest is not to irritate his readers, and who in any case is not publishing for morons, is in the last resort the best judge of where the iron should be applied.

Almost all large publishing houses have a house style for general books which they expect their printers to observe, while smaller firms rely on the printers' own rules for consistency of presentation. Almost all reputable publishing houses listen to the preferences of general authors in such matters as spelling and punctuation, either arguing the toss, or overruling eccentricities, or agreeing outright to instruct the printer to "follow copy" if the author insists. I see no reason why the scholarly editor should not submit to the same amiable discipline: and I am sure that he would the more willingly do so if he had in front of him, before he prepared his text, a set of flexible principles drawn up by a trusted academic press, and if he knew that other scholars like himself were customarily invited to observe or to discuss those principles.

I suppose that the Oxford University Press publishes more collections of authors' letters than any other firm. Some are printed in Oxford and are therefore wholly the responsibility of the Delegates of the Clarendon Press: others, printed and published in America and elsewhere, are marketed in Britain by the Press, and the responsibility of the Delegates cannot extend to the methods of editorship. But even with this limitation of responsibility it surprises me that the Delegates have not drawn up lines of guidance, if only for the benefit of their own staff of readers and copy-editors. They have a long history of scholarly publishing. They have a highly educated and trained staff who can view the scholars' problems from outside, with understanding and without prejudice. And they could enlist the expertise, and weigh the opinions, of the many living scholars whose editions they publish. They also incidentally have had, for more than half a century, in *Hart's Rules for Compositors and Readers*, the best manual of house style in the world. With all this at their back they could come up with the answer, a code, in Housman's phrase, *editorum in usum* – a code which would carry no little weight with other academic presses and commercial publishers.[1]

I was discussing the subject of editorial techniques with a scholar in Oxford not long ago. He warned me that if I said what I have been saying to you in the last quarter of an hour I should be supposed to be attacking North American scholarship. I can assure you that it is not so. I have today instanced editors from two other continents who seem to me to promote Antiliterature. And if I were to attempt to draw up a code of guidance that code – as I hope I have shown – would be heavily indebted to the policy statements of scholars working not only

1 / Since this paper was written I have learned that the Clarendon Press has such a code under consideration.

in the United States, but in the one-time province of Upper Canada. No: if I am arraigning anybody it is what I call the Eng. Lit. sector of the Ed. Biz. the world over, or a sector of that sector. And having stuck my neck out so far, I may as well go further.

The *gravamina* of the arraignment are two, both concerning what I shall be ill-bred enough to call in-breeding. First, the techniques of manuscript transcription, and also those of biblio-graphical description, are a necessary part of the discipline of the graduate student. His mastery of these techniques must be made clear to his examiners when he submits his thesis. So far, so good. But these techniques have been for several years so integral to his study and his way of thinking that he comes to regard them as vital to the book into which he hopes, possibly after further years of labour, to convert his thesis for publication. Unless discrimination of a high order has also been a part of his discipline – and it should be a task of his educators to see that it is so – he faces his potential publisher with unenviable alterna-tives: to reject his book as unprofitable though meritorious ("publishers are ordinary commercial men, and their purposes are ordinary commercial purposes") ; to accept it as meritorious though unprofitable (a prerogative, indeed, of academic presses and wealthy foundations) ; or, in academic phraseology, to "refer" it, that is to say to tell the young man, now perhaps not so young, to go away and rewrite it in a form wholly at variance with the standards to which his long training has taught him to aspire.

I speak not so much from experience of reading manuscripts of learned or semi-learned works for general publishers, though I have done this in my time, as from experience on the com-mittees of societies that set out to publish works of scholarship which no publisher, commercial or academic, is willing to undertake. All too often the merit is apparent but there has been a failure of judgment, of discrimination. Fidelity to Eng. Lit. techniques has made unpalatable something which, instead of being caviare to the general, might have been wholesome food for that wider and, if I may say so, that not altogether unintelligent reading public whose advocate I have set out to be.

My second charge is that even when the graduate student with his further degree has blossomed into full professorial status, perhaps with many years of successful research and teaching behind him, he may still regard English literature as a closed shop – may still regard the work he wishes to publish as arcane, a mystery only for initiates. The closed shop is the begetter of the unopened book.

I spoke a little while ago about "the letters of an author *or of any other man.*" It is generally true to say that it is only literary authors whose letters are edited with the same elaborate techniques as are applied to manuscripts of creative literature. To too many Eng. Lit. editors a manuscript is a manuscript. Poem or essay or novel, letter or diary or notebook, it must be given the full treatment. It is not so, or is very seldom so, with other men's letters or diaries or notebooks – the philosopher, the statesman, the physician, the soldier, the explorer. Few publishers would consider publishing these men's letters in the more extreme of the forms adopted for poets like Shelley and Keats. The reading public would not stand for it.

I shall conclude by rephrasing the four points I made earlier about Victorian publishers as censors:

(a) that the twentieth-century academic publisher should have a clear, though not rigid, personal view of how letters should be edited;

(b) that he may reasonably not wish to alienate an educated public wider than the constituency of the campus;

(c) that publishers who accept scholarly editors on trust, without having first discussed techniques with them, may be asking for trouble; and

(d) that editors who resent interference, thinking they know better than "ordinary commercial men," should beware lest, in John Murray's words with which I started, they do injustice to authors for whom they entertain the sincerest devotion.

TITLES MENTIONED

The following list comprises the editions of authors's letters referred to in the second half of this paper.

The Correspondence of Arthur Hugh Clough. Edited by F. L. Mulhauser. 2 vols. Oxford, 1957.

Collected Letters of Samuel Taylor Coleridge. Edited by E. L. Griggs. 4 vols. Oxford, 1956–59.

The Letters of Charles Dickens. Edited by M. House and G. Storey. vol. 1. Oxford, 1965.

The George Eliot Letters. Edited by G. S. Haight. 7 vols. New Haven, 1954–55.

The Letters of Mrs. Gaskell. Edited by J. A. V. Chapple and A. Pollard. Manchester, 1966.

The Letters of John Keats. Edited by H. E. Rollins. 2 vols. Cambridge, Mass., 1958.

The Rossetti-Macmillan Letters. Edited by L. M. Packer. Berkeley, 1963.

Letters of Dante Gabriel Rossetti. Edited by O. Doughty and J. R. Wahl. 4 vols. Oxford, 1965–67.

The Letters of Percy Bysshe Shelley. Edited by F. L. Jones. 2 vols. Oxford, 1964.

The Letters of Sydney Smith. Edited by N. C. Smith. 2 vols. Oxford, 1953.

The Letters of Anthony Trollope. Edited by B. A. Booth. Oxford, 1951.

The Letters of Oscar Wilde. Edited by R. Hart-Davis. London, 1962.

Reference is also made to K. Coburn, *The Notebooks of Coleridge.* vol. 1. New York, 1957.

The Canadian Author
and Publisher
in the Twentieth Century

GEORGE L. PARKER

THE SUBJECT OF THIS YEAR'S conference, the author and his relations with the publishing house, has received very little attention over the years from scholars and critics investigating Canadian writing. The reason is not hard to find; it is chiefly because the larger territory of Canadian writing has only developed as a subject for research since the 1940s. In the last ten years, for example, two works appeared which have considerably facilitated the approaches to our literary past: Professor R. E. Watters' *Check List of Canadian Literature ... 1628–1950* (Toronto: University of Toronto Press, 1959) and *The Literary History of Canada* (Toronto: University of Toronto Press, 1965), produced under the general editorship of Professor Carl Klinck. Now that there is a conference – not the first one, however – which is sympathetic to the consideration of Canadian publishing and writing, and now that Canadian literature has been officially recognized as a sub-section of Commonwealth writing by the Modern Language Association, perhaps we shall soon see closer attention given to the problems of authorship and our publishing trade during both the nineteenth and twentieth centuries.

My purpose in this short paper will be two-fold. First, I want to speak about research in this field: to survey the materials which are available, to indicate what work has been done so far, and to suggest some topics for investigation. Second, I want to spend the remaining time talking about the book situation between the 1890s and the 1920s, the period when a number of Canadian authors were successful as best-sellers in Canada and abroad, and when most of the leading contemporary Canadian publishing houses were established. With the exception of such books as Sara Jeanette Duncan's *The Imperialist* and Leacock's *Sunshine Sketches* and *Arcadian Adventures*, the two decades after 1900 do not sparkle with memorable poems and novels. Perhaps this absence explains why the period is something of a blank in Canadian literary history, in contrast to the creative moments on either side of those two decades, the 1890s and the 1920s and 1930s. After 1922, there was practically no mention of the prosperous decade before the first world war or of the spectacular publishing successes during the war. I propose today to describe a few of those events which changed the nature of the Canadian book trade and to explain why publishers and authors began to take a lively interest in each other's affairs.

A NOTE ON SCHOLARLY APPROACHES

The fragmentary nature of the raw materials which the scholar can draw on makes his investigation both frustrating and challenging. Let me classify these materials into four groups: first, author-publisher correspondence, contracts, sales records, and publishers' catalogues; second, comprehensive annual bibliographies of imprints from Canadian firms; third, subject bibliographies dealing with copyright, the book trade, and house histories; fourth, a mixed bag of monographs, reports, and trade journal articles. To what extent are the materials in these four groups available?

There is a dearth of basic materials such as letters and sales records. These have been rarely preserved, with thoroughness or regard for scholarly hunting, in the archives of publishing firms or universities or governments. There are only two good collections of publishers' letters that I know of in Canadian archives: one is the Lorne Pierce Collection at Queen's University, and the other is the Graphic Publishers' papers in the National Archives. We ought to have many more. Let me make a plea here to publishers to save their back files, and to donate or sell these to universities. Of course, there are a great many letters and records scattered throughout the country – many of them still in private hands – which should tempt the ambitious scholar with plenty of time, patience, and resources to assemble them.

With regard to the second group, we find that before 1950, when the National Library began to publish *Canadiana*, an annual bibliography of publications of Canadian origin and interest, there were no official annual records. There are, however, a number of recent compilations which list by year Canadian imprints or Canadiana, more or less covering the years 1534 to 1949.[1] These are important starting points, along with Professor Watters' *Check List*, and are probably as comprehensive as we shall ever have for the earlier years of our history, but we are still without official statistics. A useful approach is to determine how many Canadian books an individual firm has published each year, as Mr. W. Stewart Wallace has done in *The Ryerson Imprint*, and as I have done for McClelland and Stewart.[2]

As for the third group, subject bibliographies, there are now three starting points: the *Canadian Index to Periodicals*, the

1 / Frances M. Staton and Marie Tremaine, *A Bibliography of Canadiana ... 1534–1867* (Toronto: Public Library, 1934); Marie Tremaine, *A Bibliography of Canadian Imprints, 1751–1800* (Toronto: University of Toronto Press, 1952); Dorothea Tod and Audrey Cordingley, *A Check List of Canadian Imprints, 1900–1925* (Ottawa: King's Printer, 1950); *The Canadian Catalogue, 1921–1949* (Toronto: Public Libraries, 1922–1950).

2 / As an appendix to my dissertation, "The History of a Canadian Publishing House: A Study of the Relation between Publishing and the Profession of Writing, 1890–1940," University of Toronto, 1969.

Annual Check List in *Canadian Literature*, and the recently published check list by Professor Watters and Inglis Bell, *On Canadian Literature* (Toronto: University of Toronto Press, 1966). I hope to add to these a fourth: the bibliography of my dissertation, which now contains some five hundred items on nineteenth- and twentieth-century copyright problems, book publishing, and individual firms and is by no means exhaustive.

Finally, there are still too few monographs. I can think of a handful only. In the eighties there was S. E. Dawson's booklet, *Copyright in Books* (Montreal: Dawson, 1882). In 1944 there was the *Report on the Canadian Book Trade*, assembled for the Book Publishers' Section of the Toronto Board of Trade. In 1966 there was Professor Gordon Roper's revised study, "Mark Twain and His Canadian Publishers: A Second Look," in *Papers of the Bibliographical Society of Canada* (Toronto: The Society, 1966), which gives a detailed account of Canadian publishing in the late 1870s and early 1880s. Recently there have been two studies by Professor H. Pearson Gundy, *Book Publishing and Publishers in Canada Before 1900* (Toronto: Bibliographical Society of Canada, 1965), and his chapter on "Literary Publishing" in *The Literary History of Canada*. Indeed, early Canadian printers have been dealt with in more detail than have nineteenth- and twentieth-century publishers, in articles by Professor Gundy and Marie Tremaine and in book form by Aegidius Fauteux. Sessional papers from government departments and reports from special committees are useful sources of evidence about the book trade, and I have found this kind of material printed as early as 1868. Among publishers themselves, individuals such as S. E. Dawson, Dan A. Rose, George Morang, Frank Wise, Hugh Eayrs, John Morgan Gray, and Eleanor Harman have written important articles and books on Canadian publishing. The great bulk of articles, however, are contemporary accounts of seasonal events, written by the trade for the trade in periodicals such as *Books and Notions* (Toronto: 1884–87), *Bookseller and Stationer* (Toronto:

1887 –), *The Canadian Magazine* (Toronto: 1893–1939), *The Canadian Bookman* (Montreal and Toronto: 1919 –), and *Quill and Quire* (Toronto: 1935 –). Discussions of the Canadian book trade are not confined exclusively to articles in Canadian trade journals, for a search through the volumes of *Publishers' Weekly, The Critic, The Bookman,* and *Publishers' Circular* indicates that American and British journals over the last seventy-five years have taken a close interest in Canadian publishing at times when Canadian copyright problems took on international ramifications.

What has become very evident in the course of my research is the number of useful studies to be done in the Canadian book trade. I can suggest four or five here. I believe histories of individual firms would be helpful to scholars, librarians, and publishers. For example, a real challenge would be to piece together the activities of the mid-nineteenth-century publisher, John Lovell, and to make a check list of Lovell's imprints. I think we also need collections of authors' letters. Mr. Arthur Bourinot was one of the few editors to have recognized the value of publishing the letters of such poets as Archibald Lampman, Duncan Campbell Scott, and their circle. Someone should compile a list of best-sellers in Canada: such a list would show variations in Canadian reading tastes from those of the United States and Great Britain and may well indicate more popularity for Canadian books than is perhaps suspected. We need a specialist in copyright who will give us a history of this problem, as well as an analysis of some judicial decisions involving Canadian copyright, for Professor H. G. Fox's study, *The Canadian Law of Copyright* (Toronto: University of Toronto Press, 1944), is by no means an exhaustive work, valuable though it is. I think someone might do an interesting comparison of the London, New York, and Toronto editions of Canadian authors' books, with a view to determining where Canadian editions were manufactured and bound. Such a study, indeed, can be done for a number of twentieth-century British and American authors who have had Canadian imprints. I believe most useful of all would be a general history of the Canadian book trade in the nineteenth and twentieth centuries. In time, hopefully, we may have studies on the order of Clarence Ghodhes' *American Literature in Nineteenth Century England* (Carbondale: Southern Illinois University Press, 1944) and Benjamin Spencer's *The Quest of Nationality* (Syracuse: Syracuse University Press, 1957). What we sadly lack are cultural studies from the Canadian point of view.

PUBLISHERS AND AUTHORS

As I said earlier, the period from 1890 to 1920 marked the appearance of best-selling authors (Canadian, British, and American) in Canada, and the establishment of many leading Canadian publishing firms. It was also the period which saw the emergence of Toronto as the centre of English-language publishing in the country. The two chief problems for publishers, whether they were printers or distributors or entrepreneurs, were their struggles to wrest control of the Canadian market from British and American printers and publishers, and their attempts to eliminate the confusing and unjust copyright laws which in effect allowed foreigners to control their markets. By 1920 these factors had been in large measure removed in so far as the publishing of Canadian authors in their own country was concerned. To explain how the change came about, let me give you three sets of historical facts dealing with copyright, authors, and publishers, all of which are relevant to the book situation.

Every ten years during this period there was copyright legislation before parliament, the purpose of which was to make Canadian copyright laws as independent as possible of Imperial control. In 1889 a protectionist Copyright Act (52 Vict., c. 29) was passed but never made operative. Indeed, the same act was passed in each session until 1894, but was disallowed each time on the advice of the Colonial Office in London. This act was intended to repeal the Copyright Act of 1875 (38 Vict., c. 88), which Canadian publishers believed was rendered ineffective after the Imperial Copyright Act of 1886 (49 and 50 Vict., c. 33) brought the British Empire into the Berne Convention. Then in 1900 an amendment (63 and 64 Vict., c. 25) to the Copyright Act of 1875 was passed and implemented. In the 1910–11 session another copyright bill was presented to parliament; this bill was presumably based on the new Imperial Copyright Act of 1911 (1 and 2 George v, c. 46) but it also contained the same old protectionist manufacturing clauses as the 1889 act. Manufacturing clauses in local or dominion acts were in contradiction to the intentions of Imperial copyright acts ever since 1886. In 1919 and 1920 substantially the same bill was again presented to parliament. After significant modifications were made in this bill to keep Canada within the Berne Convention, the bill was finally passed in 1921, came into force in 1924, and, with further revisions and amendments, has remained the operative Copyright Act (11 and 12 George v, c. 24) in Canada.

My second set of facts concerns the profession of authorship, a phrase used here in the sense of a vocation which supports an artist financially. Professor Gordon Roper has calculated that up to 1880 about 150 Canadians published over 250 volumes of fiction, whereas "during the years 1880 to 1920, more than 400 Canadians published over 1,400 volumes of fiction."[3] I do not know if anyone has made comparable figures for volumes of poetry, but I should think there would be a rough correspondence between the figures. Through the past hundred years fiction writers, unlike poets, have made viable careers from their writing.

And still another set of facts. Here is a list of some of the new firms which were established in the years before 1914: The Westminster Company (1896), George N. Morang (1897), C. J. Musson (1898), McLeod (1898), McLeod and

3 / Gordon Roper, "New Forces: New Fiction," *Literary History of Canada*, p. 261.

Allen (1901), Oxford (1904), Macmillan (1905), Thomas
Langton (1906), McClelland and Goodchild (1906), Cassel
(1907), Hodder & Stoughton (1911), Bell & Cockburn (1911),
J. M. Dent (1913), Thomas Nelson (1913). What do all these
facts suggest? Well, I believe that the continual efforts to change
copyright legislation were indications of an important transition
in the Canadian trade. Simply stated, the problem – which was
by no means unique to Canada – was whether copyright legislation should serve the manufacturer of a book or the author.
Thus, the history of Canadian copyright for the forty years after
1890 is a confusing struggle between printing firms on the one
hand and agency publishers and authors on the other. In 1902,
when George Morang looked back on the preceding twelve
years, he said simply, " ... a Canadian publishing trade hardly
existed" in 1890.[4] He was oversimplifying, of course, since a
quick check in a Toronto directory for 1890 will uncover some
sixty firms calling themselves publishers. Morang meant that
agency and original publishing, as distinct from printing, were
not characteristic of Canadian publishing, although agency and
original publishing in Canada after 1880 were perhaps not so
rare as writers in the 1900s liked to believe. Nevertheless, the
nineteenth-century Canadian publishing trade was basically a
reprint industry and, in copyright matters, publishers believed
in the necessity for manufacturing clauses which would permit
them to supply and thereby control the Canadian market.
Such clauses would lessen their risks in printing and distributing
local editions of British and American copyrights. However,
through the dispensations of Imperial copyright acts which had
precedence over local Canadian acts for the period between
1842 and 1923, British and American publishers and jobbers
could export cheap books to Canada in such quantities and at
such low prices that Canadian publishers found themselves frustrated at every turn. They were faced, and still are, by the

4 / George N. Morang, *The Copyright Question ... to the Toronto Board
of Trade* (Toronto: Morang, 1902), p. 6.

problem of distributing books over the width of a continent to a population which has been comparable to that of the north-eastern seaboard of the United States.

By the end of the 1890s, however, there were too many forces opposing the protectionist views of both the Canadian Copyright Association and the Wholesale Booksellers' Section of the Toronto Board of Trade. British authors and publishers, the American ambassador in London, the rights of authors as recognized in the Berne Convention, the notion of publication and sale as activities distinct from printing, the principle that copyright should protect the author's work: all these forces in the end were against the Canadian supporters of the concept of copyright protection as dependent on the place of manufacture. After a decade of disputes, the Canadian Society of Authors, the Wholesale Booksellers' Section, and the printing unions agreed to a compromise amendment in the 1900 act. It gave the Canadian publisher the privilege of arranging for the manufacture of foreign copyrights, or of obtaining an exclusive license to be the sole importer of foreign copyrights. Hence, these privileges were intended to restrict the importation of books by retail booksellers and to stop foreign publishers from arbitrarily flooding the Canadian market with cheap reprints.

While it did make allowance for local manufacture of books, the amendment was really an admission that Canadian publishing could not be built up on protectionist laws. As far as I can determine, there was no really significant increase in book manufacturing after 1900. In 1905, Arthur Conrad, a journalist writing in *Bookseller and Stationer*, pointed out that "few books are entirely published in Canada, including in the term 'published', the setting up of type, the printing of the sheets and the binding of the volume."[5] Indeed, Conrad estimated that three-quarters of the books which Canadians read came from the United States. The typical publisher operated in the following ways.

5 / Arthur Conrad, "Book Publishing in Canada," *Bookseller and Stationer*, XXI (August 1905), 293.

As a rule he imported sheets at 20 per cent duty and had them bound in Canada. He might import books at 10 per cent duty, arranging with the foreign publisher to have the Canadian imprint placed in the imported copies. He might borrow or rent plates from a British or American publisher, use them in Canada, and ship them back. In short, in any of these activities the Canadian publisher might be an original publisher, an agency publisher, and, in the third situation, a reprint publisher.

Predictions of success and prosperity surrounded the arrangements for the 1900 Amendment. At an 1895 conference on copyright held in Ottawa, the discussions of which became the basis for the act five years later, John Ross Robertson, the publisher of the Toronto *Evening Telegram,* stated that "men who, before, never thought of publishing will take advantage on the provisions of this Act."[6] In a similar vein, *The Canadian Magazine* pointed out after the act was passed that it would be "the first step toward making Canadian authorship a remunerative occupation by making the business of publishing itself more remunerative."[7] Thus, the significant changes after the 1900 amendment were the appearance of the new publishing firms, and the gradual recognition by the members of the Wholesale Booksellers' Section of the need to support Canadian authors. These young publishers were entrepreneurs: sometimes agents, and sometimes managers of subsidiaries of foreign firms. In other words, they were glorified wholesale booksellers, and if they had larger ambitions, as some of these men did, they might look for a best selling MS among Canadian writers, in the hope of sharing its production costs with an American or British publisher. It is probable that John McClelland, for instance, decided to organize his own firm when he had been instrumental in getting Robert Service's *Songs of a Sourdough* (Toronto: Briggs, 1907)

6 / Canada, Copyright Question, *Conference on the Copyright Question* (Ottawa: Queen's Printer, 1896), p. 5.

7 / "Book Reviews," *The Canadian Magazine,* xv (September 1900), p. 475.

published, shortly after which he had left the employ of the Methodist Book and Publishing House.

Apparently the operation of an agency firm did not require an expensive outlay. In 1910, the short-lived *Canadian Bookman* described Canadian publishing operations thus: "our publishing business has not yet reached that degree of systematized effort, where there is one department for this and another department for that, all working harmoniously. With us it is usually a one-man affair from beginning to end, and, in the actual work of producing a book, he has no time left for advertising it."[8] In this same year, the Wholesale Booksellers reorganized themselves as the Publishers' Section of the Board of Trade. And when the Copyright Bill of 1910 was before parliament, the publishers began to speak out for authors' rights, at the same time repudiating the manufacturing clauses placed in the Bill at the insistence of the Canadian Copyright Association. What distressed agency publishers was the Bill's proposition that Canadian authors would not be granted copyright protection unless their books were made in Canada. Frank Wise, the president of Macmillan of Canada, explained why manufacturing clauses were not feasible for the Canadian book industry:

It is much to be regretted of course, that the present size of our population will not make profitable for consumption wholly in Canada the cost of type-setting and printing here a book written by a Canadian, and so, unfortunately, many a good MS is now returned to its writer because the Canadian sales will not warrant a publisher undertaking its cost of production, an American publisher not finding it of sufficient interest to his public to warrant his undertaking any part of its initial cost by publishing it in the States. This proves the Canadian publisher's contention that the mere inclusion of a "manufacturing clause" will not of itself increase the amount of printing to be done in Canada. With our population growing by such leaps and bounds as at present, the

8 / "Gossip of the Month," *Canadian Bookman*, II (March 1910), 35.

time will come when we in Canada can absorb what we produce, and for that reason we should be content to bide our time and, meanwhile, preserve our Canadian national literature, even if at present it is only potential.[9]

After the 1911 national election, the copyright question was shelved for eight years.

What does the increasing number of writers in Canada mean? We know from Mr. Lehmann-Haupt's account in *The Book in America* that in the decade following the passage of the United States Copyright Act of 1891 a number of new publishing firms appeared in the United States, and that the fiction market was at a peak just after the turn of the century. A large group of Canadians, beginning with Gilbert Parker, Ralph Connor, and William Henry Drummond, had access to American markets and their books often had spectacular international sales. Their success did much to advance the status of professional writing in Canada, to establish these authors as interpreters of Canadian society, and to convince Canadian publishers that local writers should be nurtured and protected. But most authors were not international best-sellers and their concerns were more prosaic than banking large semi-annual royalties. A weekly literary column conducted by three young Canadian poets in the Toronto *Globe* through 1892 and 1893 sheds some light on the writer's position. In this column, called *At the Mermaid Inn*, Wilfred Campbell, Archibald Lampman, and Duncan Campbell Scott constantly stressed that decade's most pressing needs: an authors' society, sympathy from the universities, and quality magazines containing serious literary criticism.

In 1899 the Canadian Society of Authors was formed. Its first concern was to press for a copyright act which would not take Canadian writers out of the Berne Convention. This possibility had been close to realization through the 1890s from

9 / Frank Wise, "Canadian Copyright," *University Magazine*, x (October 1911), 54.

pressure by the Canadian Copyright Association, which regarded the Berne Convention as an obstacle in the development
of the Canadian book-manufacturing industry. Nevertheless,
the Society was very willing to support Canadian publishers on
other matters, and the Honorable George Ross addressed the
first meeting of the Society as follows:

It must be evident that the Canadian market can be most quickly
and adequately developed by the Canadian publishers. In the
publishing business, close contact between publishers and book
buyers is essential. In no other way can the demand be properly
responded to. The effect of rendering the Canadian market a
separate one would be greatly to increase an already large demand
for books; and indirectly to promote the development of Canadian
publishing, the growth of native literature.[10]

The Society's faith in the publishers was in no small way the
result of the efforts of three publishers who had been promoting
Canadian writers with some success through the 1890s. They
were William Briggs, of the Methodist Book and Publishing
House, William Copp of Copp, Clark, and George N. Morang.
Briggs made it his policy to publish Canadian poetry, biographies, travel books, and sermons, and, after 1895, Canadian
fiction. His firm also deserves mention as the training ground for
many younger Toronto publishers. Copp made a success of
selling Gilbert Parker's *Seats of the Mighty* in a clothbound
Canadian Copyright Edition in 1896; thereafter, he enlarged
his activities by manufacturing new and reprint editions of
foreign authors as well as Canadian authors. Morang, an
American who had come to Toronto to manage Appleton's
Canadian agency, organized his own firm in the late 1890s and
began to publish Canadian textbooks. He also published the first

10 / "The Canadian Society of Authors" (1900?), typewritten MS in
John Ross Robertson's folio, *Canadian Copyright*, in the Toronto Public
Libraries.

large series in Canadian publishing, the twenty volumes of biographies, The Makers of Canada, which was jointly edited by Pelham Edgar and Duncan Campbell Scott. Morang took a deep interest in copyright matters, publishing at his own expense in 1902 two letters to authors and publishers on Canadian copyright. His firm was later merged with Macmillan of Canada. In 1905, John Cooper, the editor of *The Canadian Magazine*, paid tribute to the three publishers: "They were working in a new field, and perhaps were often pessimistic as to the outcome – especially when some of the prominent people in the country tried to throw cold water on the attempt to build up a native literature. Those days are nearly past however ..."[11]

In spite of so many improvements, the position of the author was still precarious. The publication of Ralph Connor's *Black Rock* in 1898 should have been a turning point for Canadian publishing and Canadian writing. At the request of the Westminster Company, Connor wrote *Black Rock* as a serial for *The Westminster* magazine, and the serialization was followed by book publication. The firm then made arrangements with Revell of Chicago to have the book published in the United States. The book made a fortune for the two-year-old Westminster Company, which had not intended in the first place to enter book publishing on any large scale. Indeed, Connor later proved to be a goldmine for George Doran, a former Canadian who worked with Revell for some years before establishing his own firm in 1908. Connor's novel, *The Foreigner*, provided Doran with his first big publishing success. Hence, for the Canadian book trade, *Black Rock*, and, indeed, Connor's next eight novels, became spectacular publishing facts against which all other sales could be judged. For Canadian writers, it meant that a successful career was possible in this country. However, *Bookseller and Stationer* cautioned its readers against assuming that

11 / "About New Books – Canadian Publishing," *The Canadian Magazine*, xxv (October 1905), 582.

the millenium had arrived. The editor observed in January 1905:

... it would seem that the time is not yet, when the young and ambitious writer can make a satisfactory start in Canada. Had Ralph Connor, instead of entering the ministery and securing for himself a settled income, attempted to build up a reputation, and earn a livelihood as an author in Canada, he would have found it next thing to impossible. Like his younger contemporary, Norman Duncan, he would have been compelled to shift his field of action to New York. But he overcame the disabilities of the situation by seeking a livelihood in another walk of life.

We feel confident that the time is drawing near, when we shall have living in Canada, a group of literary men, who, in point of ability, will compare favorably with the best writers of modern times. Meantime, our publishers are strengthening themselves, and broadening their field, so that in time to come they will be able to undertake the original publication of the works of Canadian authors.[12]

This note of caution was based on the knowledge that, in spite of the successes of half-a-dozen fiction writers, the average sales of many Canadian writers did not produce profits for either publisher or writer. Isabella Valency Crawford's *Collected Poems*, published by Briggs in late 1905, is a case in point. Perhaps the poems did not sell well because the author had been dead for eighteen years; nevertheless, *The Canadian Magazine* believed the reason was simply that the interest in Canadian literature, which ought to have been fostered by the universities, was almost non-existent, and echoed Wilfred Campbell's opinion of fifteen years earlier in the *Mermaid Inn* column:

... although Isabella Valency Crawford's complete volume of poems has been published near a year and a half, less than five hundred copies have been sold. One would suppose that the city of Toronto

12 / "A Canadian Literature," *Bookseller and Stationer*, XXI (January 1905), 18.

alone would have taken that number. It is really inconceivable that a volume of poetry of such qualities, which has won lengthy eulogiums from the critics, should find so inconsiderable a sale. Evidently what is needed is more attention to be given to our Canadian writers in the schools and colleges. Why should the work of the classes in literature be confined to the English and American poets, and our own be neglected? It is time our educationalists woke up to the fact that we have a literature well worthy of study. Perhaps that will come when more of the native-born begin to fill our professorial chairs.[13]

A number of Canadian books did sell extremely well at home. Here are some figures:

The Man from Glengarry (1901), a first edition in Canada of 10,000;

The Doctor (1906), a first edition in Canada of 20,000;

The Trail of '98 (1910), between 10 and 15,000 sold in the Christmas season;

Sunshine Sketches (1912), 6,000 copies sold by Christmas;

Canada in Flanders (1916), over 40,000 sold in Canada in the first four months;

The Cow Puncher (1917), 10,000 copies sold within the first month;

The Major (1917), a first edition in Canada of 30,000, and a royalty of $7,500 to Connor on publication day;

Bob Edwards' Calgary Eye Opener (1920), 30,000 sold.

During the first world war the Canadian book trade continued the yearly increasing prosperity which had characterized the years from 1899 to 1913. Every January members of the trade expressed their surprise and delight at the successful

13 / "A Lack of Appreciation," *The Canadian Magazine*, XXIX (May 1907), 98. Canadian academics were not wholly uninterested in the nation's literature. Archibald MacMechan at Dalhousie, Pelham Edgar at Victoria College in the University of Toronto, and Douglas Leader Durkin at the University of Manitoba all promoted Canadian writing.

Christmas season. The demand in Canada for books was so great that, on a number of occasions, McClelland, Goodchild and Stewart had some books manufactured in Canada and supplemented these with imported editions from both the United States and Great Britain. Firms were paying royalties of up to twenty-five per cent on their best sellers. The impact of the war and the celebration of the fiftieth anniversary of Confederation were factors which contributed to the new sense of national identity and the spirit of optimism which infused Canadian book circles in the post-war years. J. Murray Gibbon believed that the war had altered Canadian book tastes. Hugh Eayrs, who became the president of Macmillan in 1921, said, "The War did to Canadian letters what years of academic study might never have done. It taught us our place as a distinct national entity and so awoke national literature. The Canadian mind is made up of so many individual types, which are not known to British and American writers, so Canadians must necessarily express the Canadian mind."[14] And in 1918, John McClelland gave his first statement on the policy of publishing Canadian writers:

For ourselves, we may say that we are specializing as far as possible on the works of Canadian writers, and prefer to give place to a Canadian book every time. We are always on the lookout for good Canadian material, and furthermore, we go out of our way to place editions of Canadian books in both the American and British markets.

We have yet to lose a dollar on any Canadian book that we have published, and we think that we can safely say that during the past two or three years we have published at least as many books by Canadian writers as any other publishing house in Canada.[15]

14 / "Publishers are getting over the fear that putting out a Canadian book is taking a chance – Big change noticeable," *Bookseller and Stationer*, xxxviii (October 1922), 27.

15 / J. Murray Gibbon, "Where Is Canadian Literature?" *The Canadian Magazine*, L (February 1918), 338. Other firms, notably Dent, Cassell,

This is no empty publicity statement. I have taken the following figures for Canadian books published by McClelland and Stewart from the check list I have prepared, and beside these I have placed corresponding figures for Canadian books from Ryerson during the same years. I am indebted to Mr. W. Stewart Wallace for the use of his figures in *The Ryerson Imprint*:

	McClelland and Stewart	Ryerson
1917	44	9
1918	42	6
1919	27	11
1920	25	9
1921	26	6
1922	41	16
1923	40	61

Interestingly enough, it was not until 1961 that McClelland and Stewart once more began to publish annually a comparable number of Canadian books. I should point out, however, that these figures must not be taken as an indication of the full publishing activity in any one year, for both firms always carried a considerable agency list.

By 1920 Canadian publishers had made important advances in the bid to supply their markets, a situation brought about as much by two decades of prosperity as by copyright legislation. As distributors of books by foreigners, they usually acted as agents, while as distributors of books by Canadians, more and more they acted as original publishers for Canadian authors. After the war the Canadian publisher could obtain with little trouble the Canadian rights for a book from either the author or a foreign publisher acting as the agent for an author, but the Canadian publisher was rarely in a position to bargain for world

Macmillan, Musson, and Ryerson were making similar policy announcements and preparing strong Canadian lists after the war.

rights for any authors. Even in the 1960s the control of world rights by Canadian publishers is all too rare. Other areas in which Canadian publishers made advances during the 1920s were in the publishing of chap books, anthologies, school texts, and literary histories. They also published cheap reprints of contemporary authors and reprint editions of such nineteenth-century Canadian writers as Thomas Chandler Haliburton, John Richardson, and Susanna Moodie.

At the beginning, I spoke of two purposes in this paper: to explain the state of research on Canadian publishing, and secondly, to resurrect an almost unknown but lively era in Canadian publishing. It is apparent that the role Canadian publishers have played in the cultural life of this country has long been neglected and minimized: I believe this state of things is detrimental to a truly comprehensive study of our literary history. In this respect we are well behind the Americans and the British, who have long recognized the interrelation of copyright laws, a healthy national publishing industry, and professional authorship.

Press Editors
and Project Editors

FRANCESS G. HALPENNY

THIS CONFERENCE HAS HAPPENED quite fortuitously to coincide
with a vigorous critical controversy about the preparation and
presentation of large scholarly editions to which even *Time*
magazine has been a contributor. It has not escaped the attention of some followers of this current debate that one group
of people intimately concerned with the occasion for it have
scarcely been heard from: the publishers. Discreet silence from
publishers in the face of both praise and blame for their efforts
has, of course, been characteristic at any period. It has been
traditional, for instance, that a publisher does not, if he is wise,
reply to a criticism in print of one of his titles. A university press
publisher is no exception. He is accustomed to rely a great deal
for the long-term support of his publications on the creation of
a general confidence in his imprint on the part of reviewers and
readers which, whatever the shortcomings or presumed shortcomings of individual authors and editors, will ensure for the
significant books on his list their due attention. But even if the
imprint of a publishing house becomes known and respected,
the people in it and their activities are often rather a mystery

and understood only by those who have had close experience of them. This can certainly be so of university press editors, who have rightly always thought of themselves as assisting the scholar to present his work to the best advantage and therefore as being most effective when their efforts appear anonymous. It is nevertheless true that, however quietly, the more senior editors of North American university presses have now acquired an experience with scholarship and the written products of scholarship which is impressive and valuable; when recognized and sought after, it can be of undeniable help to individual authors and editors. Indeed it is because they *are* editors, and experienced in the ways of manuscripts, that they can offer aid in the planning and preparation of the large projects with which we are concerned here. It should really be no surprise, as it is no accident, that one of the most respected university press editors, Donald Jackson of Illinois University Press, recently shifted his place of operation to take up an appointment as editor-in-chief of the works of George Rogers Clark.

Part of my purpose here is to take away a little of this anonymity and to describe in general terms something of the part played by a university press in the development of editorial projects. What is said will, I hope, have the modesty yet the resolution which befits an editor.

A book is, among other things, an example of creative art and for its proper effect requires an audience. The necessary liaison between the two is provided by the publisher, who takes the author's work and gives it the form in which it reaches its audience. The publisher depends for his effectiveness on the sureness and keenness of the connection he establishes between author and audience, and must be active in maintaining the connection between the two to the best advantage of both. A university press must be no less sensitive to claims on its attention from the two groups on which scholarly publishing depends. It should be or become aware of the kinds of works which the particular audience it is addressing needs or might need in the future, and it must also be alert to respond to the contributions scholars are making or would make with the right encouragement. Editorial projects are no exception here. Sometimes the desire of the audience can be recognized by the publisher before the project that will satisfy it is in the offing. Sometimes a scholar or group of scholars will begin a project because they and others they know have been frustrated by lack of the editions they plan or have been intrigued by the content or editorial challenge of what they propose to work on. I emphasize that I exclude from this description, even if one cannot help being uneasily aware of its existence, make-work editing or publishing; it is to be found, in one extreme, in elaborately footnoted critical texts of obscure works which should have been left in thesis form, or on the other hand in collections of material, allegedly in demand and unobtainable, gathered behind a sketchy introduction and uneasily supported on a weak underpinning of notes. These exercises will be done, the pressures of academic life, which are felt all too often in publishing, being what they are; university presses can only – and because of numbers this is indeed a necessity – stiffen their resistance to them. What my remarks are rather concerned with is editorial work of the kind scholars and their publishers would like to see: carried out on documents worthy of attention; appropriate in scope to the subject; undertaken with enthusiasm and diligence; carried forward by approved and sensible scholarly methods; and presented with dignity and assurance. There may be a measure of idealism here, of course, but this kind of work must surely be the aim. If it is in some way fulfilled, the publisher should find that the audience will welcome what is being presented to it; the scholars will have collaborated to fill a need suitably; the balance I have been speaking about will be steady.

However, there is an axiom of university press publishing which deserves stating here: we must not undertake to direct research. Our responsibility is to ensure publication for worthy scholarly manuscripts which are presented to us, and especially for those which might not otherwise be published appropriately. One of the reasons for this limitation is, of course, financial. The funds we have available for assisting manuscripts can be used only for production and publication, and support for the research which creates them must come from grants to scholars by institutions set up for this purpose whether inside or outside the universities. The separation is not only necessary, it is healthy. Scholarship should be largely self-generating, the response of an individual or a group of individuals to an observed need. Research will really only be carried forward to a successful conclusion if it is initiated by some person or some group which believes firmly in the value of what is being undertaken and is able to maintain an interest in the work through the months, even years, of preparation, despite the frustrations of interruptions from other commitments or of nagging problems in the project itself. In a large editorial project patience is an essential attribute for the pursuit of details of fact or interpretation or of presentation. It takes editors with resilient and stout hearts, and, I submit, a saving sense of humour.

This point about the direction of research is valid even in connection with such an enormous commission as the multi-volume *Dictionary of Canadian Biography*. Its staff carries out research activities which have been given a large measure of financial support; its volumes would not exist, however, unless individual contributors across the country had felt impelled to join in creating this national record, and contributors' fees would not be enough in themselves to move them.

The distinction between the financial support for research and for publication which is being made here may help to explain the position which university presses must sometimes take when they receive inquiries about certain kinds of editorial projects. We are sympathetic to a scholar who comes in to ask about a one- or two-volume edition he would like to do, and wants our commitment to it. He is reluctant to embrace the dust and heat of preparation unless he can see publication across the plain, and he perhaps wonders about an advance. We must usually reply that the sort of edition he has in mind will undoubtedly require assistance for publication, and that funds can be made available for this purpose only, and only on the basis of a final manuscript which has been approved by qualified readers. The impetus to proceed must come from his own interest in the project. What we *are* able to say is whether the project he outlines seems valuable or not, and we may seek outside opinion on this point. By this means an unpromising activity can be identified and the project halted or else revised in a way that holds promise for publication when completed. Necessary caution can in these circumstances be helpful in the long run through the advice given to the scholar by the press editor.

I would not for a moment wish it to be felt that university presses are unaware of or unsympathetic to the need for support for research. We are indeed as anxious as any scholar that the funds available for it should be increased. We are all too aware of the hindrances to effective work which episodic investigation and interrupted writing or editing can cause. A manuscript will inevitably be less effective if its author has had to do the reading and writing for it in fits and starts during academic sessions, with bouts of concentration in the summers and little opportunity for connected and continuous reflection. Press editors, always aware of projects they would like to see completed or even started, and faced all too often with the unhappy effects of delay on the manuscript itself, would agree with me, I am sure, in saying that quality would be likely to improve greatly if an author or editor were able to take sensible allowances of time supported by adequate funds for living and for securing such aids as typing, xeroxes, microfilms, and junior research assistance. He would, hopefully, maintain his keenness in exploring his subject and an editorial committee could have greater alacrity in pursuing the fine points of its textual criticism instead of having to combat lethargy, forgetfulness about details of what has been done, subtle and perhaps unrecognized changes of direction over time, and the boredom that comes from having to take up again and again what never seems to get completed. It would seem entirely possible that not only would the results be better scholarship, but readers would have them sooner and authors and editors could accomplish more both in research and in teaching. As you see, this statement on greater support for research makes no distinction between works of criticism and critical texts, and this would seem to be fair, if all projects of either sort are valid ones.

However, there surely is reason to wonder whether validity of aim or method is always adequately checked when research funds are being allocated. Press editors have been known to feel restive indeed when confronted by projects planned for an audience a publisher is going to have to look much too hard to find or which seem to be using over-elaborate, or unnecessarily tiresome and time-consuming methods for results that may not warrant the effort, or when they are invited to consider manuscripts presented as almost final by those submitting them but which the editor discovers have been initiated without adequate knowledge of the scholarly traditions of their kind (for instance, in the handling of an edition of letters or the presentation of a large body of references). None of us would suggest that projects should have publishing scrutiny, much less approval, as part of the consideration before research grants are made. This would be undesirable for many obvious reasons: the presses might well be wrong in their judgments, no two presses are exactly alike in their publishing programmes or their editorial reactions, and scholarship must be free to follow its inspirations and insights at all times. What we do wish, and here the wish is surely legitimate, is that those who are embarking on larger projects, in particular, would seek whatever opportunity they may have to discuss them with a senior university press editor and see whether some comment can be made which will bear upon the preparation of the manuscript for publication.

To this point I shall return shortly, but I should like to continue here with the question of finance, this time as it affects the fate of a project within the press. In his article in *Editing Eighteenth-Century Texts* on the edition of Samuel Johnson, Donald Greene refers to the refusal of several presses to take an interest in it. I do not know the identity of these presses, and am certainly ignorant of their reasons for declining. Perhaps they were simply obtuse or frightened as Mr. Greene's statement rather implies. We make mistakes, just as scholars do. But there is another aspect to be considered. Projects such as the Johnson or the More or the Mill or any one of the American Authors represent an enormous publishing investment for any press, and an investment which is likely to be spread over a goodly number of years. The size of the investment comes from the considerable editorial contribution in planning and in superintending manuscript and proof; in the requirement for careful design of what is often a variety of materials; in the sheer bulk of the typesetting with its panoply of complications in notes, footnotes, signs, appendices, introductions, and indices; in the necessity for rigorous checking of what is typeset and proofed. Against these production figures must usually be set the fact that sales will not be of comparable proportions, that if the list price of volumes is set too high sales to individuals will be affected, but that in any case most sales will be to libraries and institutions, and that these will not often be enough to do more than cover running costs (that is, the cost of presswork and binding only). Moreover, these sales will tend to occur slowly. Reviews take months to appear in North America, and they may not be available until well after publication. At the beginning, the publisher will thus be depending largely on his standing orders. The sales will likely keep up at a steady rate and will have a spurt as a new volume is added to the series, but the rate will be such that the publisher is maintaining an expensive inventory over some little time and must also be prepared to reprint as need arises. In short, what we are describing is a non-commercial undertaking, and the press must find somewhere the subsidy that will be required to make it possible. (It is worth noting here that although huge sums were originally planned for the preparation of the American Authors series, no part of the funds is available for publication.)

For subsidy a press normally turns to the funds allotted to it to support its scholarly publishing. And it is here that the crucial point in a decision to publish is reached. The investment involved in a large editorial project could simply pre-empt those funds, making it necessary for the press to curtail its other scholarly publishing. Some such limitation might be possible, of course, but would not be acceptable for long. Let me take the Collected Works of John Stuart Mill as an example. When the University of Toronto Press began this project, it did so after concluding that its Publications Fund (which supports its subsidized publishing) was strong enough to take the additional commitment of the series; indeed, the academic committee investigating the feasibility of the edition made the ability of the Fund to assume it without hindrance to the Press's other scholarly publishing a contingency in its recommendations. The planning of the series, in which both editorial and publishing considerations fitted together in the happiest manner, brought Francis Mineka's eagerly awaited text of the *Earlier Letters* and then a key work, the *Principles of Political Economy*, out first, and the arrangement of the contents of the volumes of essays now appearing is such that they can be directed to both a particular audience of individuals and libraries. But even with all these aids, and excellent reviews, and the sale of an English edition, the Press's Fund will not receive back much more than the running costs of these volumes. In the next several years, it has to contemplate a large volume of essays, the two volumes of the *Logic* and four volumes of *Later Letters* totalling some 2,000 pages. It was clear that its Fund could only cope with this advance upon it by delaying publication of some volumes for an unacceptable time. The Canada Council has fortunately now given a grant for the *Essays on Ethics, Religion, and Society* and for the *Logic* and this timely help should enable the Press to proceed with later volumes on its own resources and helped by the increasing sales from more volumes in print. I relate this experience simply to show something of the circumstances that must be taken into account in embarking on projects of this kind. We find those circumstances stimulating rather than dour, and feel only satisfaction in what the collaboration of editorial and publishing planning has succeeded in doing so far. But caution has to be maintained at all stages.

Having introduced the editorial aspect, let me turn now to some comments on the collaboration of the two sets of editors. It can occur, of course, at a variety of times and in a variety of ways. One of them is in consultation when a project is just coming together. Indeed, as suggested earlier, the senior press editors may assist in helping the future collaborators to assemble in the first place. Though they do not presume to direct research, they would not be publishers' editors in any true sense of the word if they were not aware of needs expressed by readers, of possibilities for works that have remained unexamined for one reason or another, of scholars working at several places who might be linked in a promising collaboration. Their offices, their visits to learned gatherings and lecture series, their reading around in their fields, are all means by which such possibilities reveal themselves. Thus, by correspondence, by conversation and consultation, by providing a site and encouragement for a group to meet to discuss a possible project, they may well find their middle place between scholar and reader an active cross-roads. It is still true, however, that the decision to proceed with a project must ultimately be taken firmly by the scholars themselves, must be defined by them, and must in largest part have its principles of operation set by them. It is on the basis of their enthusiasm and on their capabilities and integrity as scholars that the publisher makes his crucial initial decision to proceed, though he reserves the right to approve individual volumes as they are completed, and it is on these factors that the success of the project finally depends. The publisher can be guide and adviser for the scholarly editors. His editor can comment on proposals, can remind the planners of the importance of determining an audience and keeping it in view at all times, and can try to ensure that the printed form in which the project is going to be presented is visualized early enough so that any implications for the scholarly editing will be seen and followed. To this kind of activity they can bring their professional competence at judging manuscripts which has likely been strengthened at one time or another in the course of their work by their consultation of what are considered to be scholarly models.

It would be rash to suggest that press editors have all the answers even in the most practical matters of printing detail. They do not, and may have to work their way out of some confusion at the beginning. But we do submit that communication by scholarly editors with press editors at all stages can be of great assistance to a large project. The early investigation of page layouts and sample settings, for instance, will be likely to reveal advantages and disadvantages in certain typefaces in accommodating neatly the apparatus for variant readings or note numbers or cross-references, and it is well to submit the most daunting section of prepared text available for this sort of experiment. The typeface should, of course, be an attractive one but it may well be that one which seems pleasing will be unable to cope with the intricacies of a critical text or can do so only at an unhappy cost in legibility. These early samples make it possible to get the "feel" of the ultimate printed page and can tell the scholarly editors a good deal about practical procedures and how much can be put on that page and still leave it coherent.

Similarly, it will be the better part of wisdom if the scholarly editors will early on let the press editors have a good sample of the typescript they are preparing. There are many points of detail that may turn out to be important. One would have thought that the messages about "double space for everything" and "please type footnotes in double space in a separate section even if they are to be printed at the bottom of pages" would be superfluous but it is unfortunately not so. Then there is the question of typing and marking certain kinds of texts with the printer in mind from the beginning so that they need not be gone over again by a press editor; it is surely easier to follow an agreed-upon form when the final manuscript is typed from the drafts, and saves much labour later. This method worked well with the *Wellesley Index*, for instance. On the basis of a discussion of order of items within the entries and an excursion with sample typesettings, the form and appearance of the entries was agreed on before the final typescript was done, and no marking for the entries was required of the press editor. I shall never forget one manuscript from a large project of bibliography, which opened its entries with an author's name. These names had all been typed in full capitals, and it was thus impossible for anyone consulting it to know what spelling would be correct if he were going to write, say, Mackenzie, in upper and lower, or a name beginning with Le and La. In a country such as Canada this is a serious confusion. Since there was no way of checking most of these names, short of returning to the library cards scattered across the country, they had to be set in full capitals and I am sure there must have been imprecations loud and deep from readers. To take a further example, a many-volumed critical edition has to face the problem of how it is going to handle cross-references in early volumes to those volumes it will not publish until later. And of course there is the question of establishing a useful style in footnote references or of urging editors of letters to make their index on the manuscript as they go so that they can have a running guide to where they have annotated the multitude of names that occur and can keep their annotations consistent in form. These are only a few indications of the many kinds of questions which are best brought up early in any editorial project large or small, and in which a press editor should be a consultant. The aim is to anticipate problems and to sort out procedures so that typescript will resemble printed page as nearly as possible and will not have to be pored over by the house editor and perhaps sent back with many questions to the academic editor. The relief of strain for the project editors can be considerable, and the saving in press time helps with those heavy production costs.

These remarks have been rather general in scope and in part, therefore, are intended as a form of introduction to what my fellow contributors to this panel will say on more specific aspects of university press involvement with large projects. But whether what we have to say is general or particular in its reference, its informing message is the same: our enthusiasm for collaboration to the best possible scholarly end.

WAYLAND W. SCHMITT

I ONLY WISH Miss Halpenny's remarks had been even more general, since I'm afraid I shall be forced to reiterate many of the points she has stated so cogently – and some of those made by Mr. Nowell-Smith as well. I find myself considerably refreshed and reassured by the widespread agreement I have found at this conference, in both the formal sessions and informal discussions, about the problems university presses and scholars must confront if they are to continue to function effectively. But at this point I should like to discuss, very briefly, the special contributions a press editor can and should make to large editorial projects directed by committees of well-established scholars.[1]

1 / Professor Schoeck's later discussion of the need for precise definition of the elements and operations of such projects is of course very relevant

I suppose there is no need to point out to anyone here that the Yale Press is involved in a considerable number of such projects. During the first conference Richard Sylvester presented a summary of the work of the St. Thomas More Project,[2] and last year Donald Greene described the workings and progress of the Yale Edition of Samuel Johnson.[3] The Franklin papers have been appearing regularly, the new edition of *Poems on Affairs of State* is gradually nearing completion, and the production of hitherto unpublished material of Jonathan Edwards is slowly getting underway. Much of the work on such editions is carried out in offices in the Yale Library, which are usually termed "factories" (the Boswell factory directed by Professor Pottle being perhaps the best known, though, interestingly enough, the Boswell papers are published by a commercial house[4]). These offices employ relatively small editorial and secretarial staffs on a full-time basis; in most cases responsibility for each volume or aspect of a particular edition is assigned to a specific scholar, frequently not a member of the Yale faculty. The activities of everyone connected with the edition are supervised by a general or executive editor, who acts largely as a spokesman for the ultimate authority: a committee of interested scholars which meets regularly to discuss problems at every level.

Without going into detail about the working arrangements of each particular project published by the Yale Press, I should say at the outset that the system I have described is a remarkably effective means for making full use of the contributions recognized scholars can make to the resolution of detailed as well as general problems concerning a multi-volumed critical edition. Nevertheless, I believe the press editor should be alert to a particular danger inherent in such a specialized organization:

---

to my remarks, throughout which I use the term "editorial committee" as a broad catchall.

2 / See *Editing Sixteenth-Century Texts* (Toronto, 1966), pp. 7–10.

3 / See *Editing Eighteenth-Century Texts* (Toronto, 1968), pp. 92–123.

4 / Mr. Greene comments on this point interestingly; see *ibid.*, p. 97.

since any scholarly committee is in essence a very small and relatively self-enclosed society, devised on the basis of a deep commitment to the most adequate and appropriate presentation of
works of a particular author (or period) with whom it is already
thoroughly familiar, it may operate according to assumptions
and interests which correspond less closely to those of the wider
public than its members realize. Whenever the committee does
in fact appear to have lost touch with certain important considerations, the press editor should be ready to assume the role
of the ultimate user of the edition, described by Professor Greene
as "the Australian reader of the year 2000." His word cannot be
final, of course, but the very fact that he has no specialized
knowledge enables him to consider the edition as a source of
relevant information – and perhaps even of pleasure – rather
than a repository of raw data. From the very outset he should
call to the attention of the committee any aspect of the project
which seems to him confused, meaningless, or downright mis-
taken.

From the editor's point of view, the central question about a
critical edition may be the nature and size of the audience to
which it is directed. This is obviously crucial to the press in determining such mundane details as prices or print orders, but it is
also related to a surprising number of specific editorial questions.
Any group of devoted scholars may believe, quite understand-
ably, that the interest in their labours is very wide; the press
editor should never hesitate to point out that the specialized
audience may be far smaller than they realize and that if the
edition is in fact meant to reach a more sizeable audience, some
modifications of editorial policy may be necessary. Above all, if
the edition is unquestionably directed toward the small group of
scholars who insist that all variant readings must be presented,
that textual and factual annotation must be complete, and that
the peculiar characteristics of the original copy should be indicated wherever possible, that fact should be faced from the

outset, so that all operations – from copy editing and production to sales and promotion – can be carried out appropriately. Much of the current confusion about the MLA editions of American authors could be mitigated, I believe, if scholarly editors and publishers as well as reviewers recognized the need to develop clear definitions of their basic functions and to defend the resulting standards and practices relentlessly. No amount of mournfulness or ill will from any party in the dispute should encourage the misguided belief that the interest of general readers – those who depend solely on the critical judgments of the *Times Book Review*, *Time* magazine, or even *The New York Review* – should be expected or solicited when an edition is not in fact intended for their purposes.

However, when an editorial committee believes that its edition should appeal to a relatively broad audience – one including at least undergraduate as well as graduate students – a number of technical problems must be faced at the very outset. Here again the press editor, acting as the future Australian reader, should express any discomfort he feels, especially when confronted with a text filled with the "barbed wire" of technical symbols. I'm sure I needn't provide any further examples of this difficulty, since it has been more than adequately discussed in Lewis Mumford's review of the published format of Emerson's journals and was most pertinently analyzed in Mr. Nowell-Smith's paper; furthermore, I know that Mrs. Kewer has some penetrating remarks concerning it. My point is simply that whenever a group of scholars loses sight of the fact that the sort of technical question which can absorb their attention (sometimes analogous to the abstract fascination of a double-crostic) may well seem meaningless or even irritating to an outsider who has been forced or encouraged to read a work for its literary or intellectual merits, the press editor must remind them of that fact. The preparation of a popular as well as a scholarly edition of some material – as in Yale's publication of both the Selected and Complete Works of St. Thomas More – may be the best solution in many cases. But, whatever plan is devised, neither the editorial committee nor the publishing press should be surprised to discover that some of the most tormenting editorial cruxes seem esoteric and inconsequential to non-initiates. Once again, a clear functional definition will provide firm support for whatever procedures they have chosen.

Miss Halpenny has already mentioned, and Mrs. Kewer will describe in greater detail, the helpful advice press editors and designers may provide concerning the amount of supplementary apparatus to be included in an edition and whether it can best be presented in footnotes or separate appendixes, or perhaps eliminated entirely from the printed volume.[5] I shall merely add that the press editor may occasionally wish to suggest that certain kinds of biographical, historical, or bibliographical data, especially those which almost automatically form a "running commentary," could more appropriately be presented in the form of a critical monograph. He may even be able to strengthen his case by suggesting that his press would be willing to consider such a study for publication, thereby increasing the size or substance of his list even as he frees the edition of clutter. I suspect that this strategy is particularly useful in confronting the problem of "evanescent" annotation, such as that mentioned by Professor Greene concerning the relevance of Samuel Johnson's political debates to certain social and political problems in contemporary America.[6] In such instances the press editor's attitude may even serve to relieve the scholarly committee of a delicate psychological problem, for everyone connected with an edition

5 / The possibility of storing supplementary or evidential material in library files or on microfilm was mentioned during the discussion which followed the papers. This practice should, I believe, be explored and encouraged by both publishers and academic editors, bearing in mind that any selected or edited version should include a clear notice of the availability of further data.

6 / See *Editing Eighteenth-Century Texts,* pp. 107–8n.

must of course be concerned with the tender care of each editor's individual temperament and interests.

On another level, the press editor may sometimes argue that certain types of manuscript, or even printed material, have enough intrinsic interest to warrant publication in facsimile form, usually with a straightforward transcript. We are currently preparing a facsimile of St. Thomas More's Prayer Book – the annotated pages from the Book of Hours and Psalter he possessed while he was imprisoned in the Tower – which we are certain will be of considerable interest to scholars, bibliophiles, and many general readers; some of the textual material in that edition will of course also be included in the Complete Works of More. Viking recently issued *Giocamo Joyce* in facsimile, and it seems certain that a photographic reproduction of the early drafts of *The Waste Land* will soon be available. While it is somewhat difficult to gauge the value and appeal of such reproduction, no publisher should overlook the possibility that it may be the most effective means of presenting certain types of material.

One further problem which must be of primary concern to the press editor is that of consistency throughout a multi-volume project prepared and published over a considerable period of time. Although the guidelines concerning the selection of copytext, the amount and type of annotation, and degree of editorial modernization or Americanization must be flexible enough to allow each individual editor some initiative, and to take account of the idiosyncratic problems presented by each particular text, the ultimate user of the edition should never be expected to recognize the momentary value of *ad hoc* procedures; if he cannot perceive a consistent set of general principles in force throughout all the volumes available to him, he will legitimately complain that the editing is haphazard if not slipshod. Above all, the press editor should insist that, no matter how anxious the editorial committee may be to see the first volume in print, it should in no way represent a tentative first step toward the final rules of procedure but must exemplify as many of them as are relevant to it. The pressure to publish will undoubtedly continue throughout the life of the project, but at no point should the editorial principles established at the outset be sacrificed to it. And I suppose there is no need to dwell on the confusion that will ensue if those principles are not in fact firmly set forth at the earliest possible moment.

In this respect, I cannot over-emphasize the importance of the guidance provided by a firm, tactful, and clearminded general editor. The value of the sort of "brainstorming" carried out by any editorial committee can be realized only by skilful leadership, and any press considering a large-scale edition should make certain that it has full faith in the administration of the project. This may seem a truism, but I suspect that it is too often overlooked when a particular proposal is supported by a large and often somewhat heterogeneous group of scholars. In any case, I should like to conclude by citing a point Richard Sylvester made to me when he learned that I was planning to attend this conference: if possible, the general editor and his "factory," if there is any, should be located on the same campus as the publishing press, and, ideally at least, he and the press editor should have regular working contacts, some of them concerned with matters other than the edition itself. All sorts of problems can be effectively and expeditiously settled if the two editors are able to communicate straightforwardly, and the advantages of keeping complex conferences or correspondence to a minimum are obvious. If nothing else, clearcut co-operation between academic and press editors can prevent the disastrous production delays that afflict far too many large-scale critical editions. That the publication of such editions is in fact best understood as a collaborative enterprise appears to be the recurrent theme of this conference, and I hope that I, like my fellow panelists, have clarified some particular aspects of the contributions press editors can make to the undertaking.

ELEANOR D. KEWER

CASE HISTORIES IN THE CRAFT OF THE PUBLISHER'S EDITOR,
CULMINATING IN A JUSTIFICATION OF BARBED WIRE

WHEN MISS HALPENNY, Mr. Kefauver, Mr. Schmitt, and I
came together shortly before the opening of the conference, I
was impressed once more by the common understanding among
university press people – an understanding based upon common
problems and common experiences, and one that has produced
a heart-warming fellowship among members of the guild. One
concomitant of this state of affairs, however, was that to our
amusement (I won't say dismay) we found that we were all
prepared to emphasize the same points in discussing the publisher's role (or that of his editor) in guiding the project initiated
by scholars toward effective presentation to its proper audience.

Since Miss Halpenny has so thoughtfully and completely
covered the field, and Mr. Schmitt has made clear two of the
very important functions of the publisher's editor – helping to
determine the audience for the work in hand and helping to
shape the work for successful address to that audience – I have
hastily rejected all the general observations I had assembled and
decided to restrict my remarks to a series of case histories from
the experience of Harvard University Press, illustrating some
small things our editorial department has done in attempting to
steer our scholarly editions of texts toward the readers they are
intended to serve.

One matter we came to consider was the book's first few
minutes in the hands of a reader. The characteristic table of
contents still found in numerous collections of letters, running

something like this: "Introduction, Short Title List, THE LET-TERS, Biographical Directory, Index," even when followed by a ten- or twelve-page listing of letters with date and recipient, somehow seemed neither to edify nor to allure. We suggested breaking the mass into subdivisions, with dates and, where feasible, with descriptive titles. Professor Elting Morison, in the Theodore Roosevelt letters, improved on this suggestion by dividing the eight-volume series into two-volume units, each with a title and an introductory essay: "The Years of Preparation, 1868–1900," "The Square Deal, 1900–1905," "The Big Stick, 1905–1909," and so on; and within each pair of volumes he subdivided further, taking special pleasure in titling some of these chapters in T.R.'s own words: "It has been a great session" (November 1905–January 1906); "Taft will carry on the work" (June 1908–November 1908). His innovation, pointed out by the Press editors to Professor Thomas H. Johnson, was adopted wholeheartedly; Mr. Johnson's chronological subdivisions of Emily Dickinson's letters were all given titles in Emily Dickinson's own words with (I think) a most attractive table of contents as a result: " ... the Hens lay finely ... " [1842–1846]; "I am really at Mt. Holyoke ... " [1847–1848]; "Amherst is alive with fun this winter ... " [1849–1850]; " ... we do not have much poetry, father having made up his mind that its pretty much all *real* life ..." [1851–1854]. Mr. Johnson also supplied brief (and charming) introductory comments carried on the verso of the chapter half-title, placing the letters in the context of E.D.'s emotional and intellectual development.

The Theodore Roosevelt letters had called our attention to another problem. Some of T.R.'s letters were a dozen or more pages long; others were very short. Since in the interest of economy we had long ago abandoned the renumbering of footnotes page by page, we asked Mr. Morison to number his notes letter by letter, to have the notes typed separately from the text, and to submit the manuscript with the notes for each letter following the letter to which they pertained. But we were still thinking in terms of footnotes and, while the twelve- or fifteen-page letters offered no problems, when three short letters appeared on the same page we sometimes had three notes numbered one below the last line of text. Almost without exception ever since, we have urged placing the notes at the end of each letter instead of at the foot of the page. The reader quickly becomes accustomed to this arrangement and seems not to be troubled by the appearance of a block of small type in the middle of the page. Pursuing our policy of co-operating with the printer for reasons of economy, we soon suggested that notes be typed on yellow paper to make it easier to separate them from the text for typesetting.

When volume I of *The Letters of James Fenimore Cooper* arrived, the notes were all nicely double-spaced on yellow paper, but letter 1, from the ten-year-old schoolboy Cooper to his father, was less than a page long while the notes ran to almost a dozen pages. Father, mother, Cooperstown, Cooper, his brothers mentioned in the letter, his schooling – all were discussed in footnotes. Our editor asked Mr. Beard if he could put most of the background material into an introduction to the first chronological division. He seized upon the idea and from volume I on he divided the letters into chronological chapters, gave them informative titles (with dates, of course), and provided a short introduction to each. (For these introductions, by the way, he used blue paper, and for the short-title list and the index of correspondents for each volume he used pink.) A good bit of the welcome informative matter was put into these little introductory essays instead of overburdening the notes. Similar brief introductions have become a characteristic of many of our collections of documents.

Our experience with the Cooper letters taught us another lesson. The volumes were published two at a time, and each volume was provided with an index of correspondents. All along we had looked forward to a comprehensive subject-and-name index to appear in the final volume. This was finally achieved, and we think it an exceedingly good index, but it cost nearly a year's delay in the publication of volumes v and vi. We are now cautioning our editors of multi-volume projects to index as they go along. This does not mean that we contemplate putting a complete index in each volume – that would be a duplication of effort and an additional expense – but, besides being a useful tool to the editor as he is working on his manuscript, an index kept up in the course of the progress of the work will make it possible to produce the final index in much less time than Mr. Beard found necessary for the compilation of his index to a six-volume series. We have recently recommended for one projected series of letters that each volume contain an index of all proper names, not only those of correspondents.

Throughout, as I have already intimated, one of our considerations has been economy – to hold prices for our public down as far as possible. We have therefore tried wherever we can to facilitate the work of the printer without impairing the effectiveness of the book for its purpose. I well remember one of my first experiences in this connection. During the second world war, when we were producing Gordon Ray's *Letters of William Makepeace Thackeray*, I was startled by an anguished cry from the Printing Office: "We are setting this on the new linotype machine, and we haven't any letters with lines through them!" This was my first real encounter with problems of cancelled matter in the machine age.

Since Mr. Ray was serving in the navy at the time and hence was unavailable for counsel, we consulted Professor Howard Mumford Jones, who was handling the proof for him. With suggestions from an old hand in the composing room and Mr. Jones's assent, we decided to enclose the cancelled matter between daggers, which the linotyper could set from his keyboard. This experience gave us a relatively inexpensive means of handling one of the problems frequently met in reproducing manuscripts.

As other groups of letters came in, however, we felt that we needed symbols having direction: Hyder Rollins' *Letters of the Keats Circle* and John Ward Ostrom's *Letters of Edgar Allan Poe* used angles – actually mathematical symbols for "less than" and "greater than," but these were unpleasantly conspicuous, and in Mr. Morison's *Letters of Theodore Roosevelt*, we settled on the shallow angle brackets that have become almost standard with us as a means of indicating matter crossed out by the writer. They are used in Mr. Rollins' Keats letters, in the Cooper and Longfellow letters, and in the Emerson journals. The cancelled matter is shown unambiguously, right where it was originally, without the necessity of an editorial interpolation, a footnote, or a textual note at the end of the volume.

Now I should like to turn to the further use of symbols – the "barbed wire" that has been so vehemently deplored by Mr. Lewis Mumford, Mr. Edmund Wilson, and others.

Let me recall that in the stimulating first paper of this conference Mr. Nowell-Smith, decrying the over-literal rendering of texts, made an important distinction between "creative" composition, which, he admitted, did merit studying in detail, and writing done for the purpose of communicating ideas to others. He pointed out, quite fairly, that the meticulous following of slips of the pen, errors in spelling, and even cancellations, impedes communication and interferes with the reader's reception of the writer's message. This conclusion is a sound one – but, in giving us his two categories of texts to be edited, he has provided the basis for a reply.

Mr. Rollins' edition of the Keats letters, singled out by Mr. Nowell-Smith for criticism, actually falls into the first category – the study of the mental processes of a creative writer. Mr. Rollins endeavoured to show Keats's mind in action: his hesitation, his second thoughts, even – in the characteristic misspellings – his probable mispronunciations. To the serious student of a man's mind these things have considerable interest. Mr. Rollins addressed his scholarly edition to students of Keats rather than to the layman; he provided more material for study than a "clear text" would have presented. Nevertheless, selections from his text are constantly in demand for use in anthologies, readers, critical studies, and other publications aimed at a wider audience. Our permissions department receives a steady flow of requests for permission to reproduce bits and pieces from the Rollins volumes.

The prickles and barbs in the Keats letters, however, are trivial as compared with those in the Emerson journals, which have been specifically attacked by the aforementioned critics who have obviously misunderstood the purpose of the edition. The classification of the Emerson journals as "creative" composition rather than "communication" is completely justified. Emerson almost always carried a notebook of some kind with him – sometimes a little pocket diary, sometimes only a few pieces of folded paper stitched together – in which to jot down his observations and his reflections. Later, reading his notes over and pondering them, he made additions, deletions, and other changes. Then from time to time he copied some of the material into another notebook where he combined it with thoughts recorded in other jottings, working toward the development of a poem, a lecture, or an essay. Thrifty Yankee that he was, he used some of his notebooks over and over again – filling them from front to back, then from back to front; sometimes writing over what was already on the page, sometimes erasing some material and using the pages for a totally different subject. (The beginnings of a poem have been discovered under some comments on his fruit trees.) Our editors are trying to present in type the contents of more than 180 of these notebooks – fragile volumes of widely varying sizes and shapes, now on the shelves of the Houghton Library. Certainly these records of Emerson's thoughts over many years of his life – the cancellations and alterations, the list of alternative words with no final choice indicated – all have meaning for the serious student who is interested in the process by which Emerson's observations, intuitions, ideas, notions, were developed into coherent form for communication.

The manuscripts themselves are not easy to read. Only through long and intensive study with various technical aids have the editors been able to untangle the layers of Emerson's jottings to present a fairly continuous transcript of one series at a time – poetry or philosophy disentangled from apple trees. In some cases recovery has been only partial, but the shards from their diggings are preserved because they may sometime be fitted together to make a significant whole.

The aim of our editors has been to make this record available to larger numbers of Emersonians than could ever hope to decipher the manuscript journals themselves. Their hope has been to enable the reader to follow Emerson – as nearly as possible – in his thinking as he struggled to work out an idea or perceived something in a sudden flash. To achieve this purpose called for a technique quite different from that used for the finished product of disciplined thought.

The problem of presenting this difficult material in type required the careful pre-planning mentioned by Miss Halpenny. The material was studied by the senior editor, the designer, and the Press editor for more than two years before the manuscript of the first volume was in final shape. From the outset we recognized that an intricate manuscript cannot be successfully imitated in type; it can only be translated. The three of us agreed that the printed texts must be relatively easy for the reader to follow, relatively inexpensive for the printer to set, and as accurate and faithful a translation of the manuscript as possible. We agreed that no attempt would be made to copy the journal page in the physical placing of the material except when there was no other way to indicate something of significance. None of us wanted to interrupt the reader in his following of Emerson's jottings by footnotes saying "Cancelled," "Interlineated," "Inserted but crossed out."

Hence the "barbed wire." With the help of the designer and the publisher's editor the scholarly editors studied the big red linotype book and chose symbols that could be set with the text on the linotype machine – symbols so easy to interpret that after the appearance of volume I Professor Gilman was congratulated by several of his colleagues on its readability. Cancellations are enclosed in shallow angle brackets. Interlineations are indicated at the beginning by an arrow pointing upward and at the end by one pointing downward. Emerson's square brackets are distinguished by being heavier than those of the editor. Where Emerson failed to choose among alternative words written above (and below) one another, the editors have assumed responsibility for the sequence and present the words in a series on the line, separated by solidi. The use of these few easily remembered devices has restricted the textual notes recording changes from Emerson's manuscript to less than two and a half pages in any volume of the six so far issued.

Eventually, the editors plan to publish selected passages from the journals for the more general reader – passages in which there will be little or no "barbed wire." Meanwhile it seems to them (and to us at Harvard University Press) that this carefully recovered scholarly text is worth all the labour it is requiring. To quote the introduction (I, xxxiv), "It is the premise of this edition that Emerson's first thoughts, the hardheaded things written for himself only, the personalia, sometimes even the false starts and unfinished sallies of thought, as well as the things that did go into the essays – all these are real facts to be valued along with the finished works in the study of Emerson, and all are needed for the revision of Emerson's reputation."

TITLES MENTIONED

The following books are all Harvard University Press publications.

The Letters and Private Papers of William Makepeace Thackeray. Collected and edited by Gordon N. Ray. 4 vols. 1945–46.

The Letters of Edgar Allan Poe. Edited by John Ward Ostrom. 2 vols. 1948.

The Keats Circle: Letters and Papers. Edited by Hyder Edward Rollins. 2 vols. 1948

The Letters of Theodore Roosevelt. Selected and edited by Elting E. Morison. 8 vols. 1951–54.

The Letters of Emily Dickinson. Edited by Thomas H. Johnson. 3 vols. 1958.

The Letters of Henry Wadsworth Longfellow. Edited by Andrew Hilen. Vols. I–II–. 1966–.

The Letters of John Keats. Edited by Hyder Edward Rollins. 2 vols. 1958.

The Letters and Journals of James Fenimore Cooper. Edited by James Franklin Beard. 6 vols. 1960–1968.

The Journals and Miscellaneous Notebooks of Ralph Waldo Emerson. Edited by William H. Gilman, George P. Clark, Alfred R. Ferguson, Merrell R. Davis, Merton M. Sealts, Harrison Hayford. Volumes I–. 1960–.

WELDON KEFAUVER

WHEN MISS HALPENNY wrote to me to suggest what I might talk about today, she indicated that she thought it would be of interest to this assembly to hear one of the publishers of the editions of American authors, proceeding under the auspices of the Center for Editions of American Authors of the Modern Language Association of America, discuss his position in the controversy raging for the past several months in the *New York Review of Books* (and only recently extended to the pages of *Time* magazine) over the value of such editions in preserving the American literary heritage.

It was tempting to indulge myself in a discussion of the definitive edition as public issue – for this it seems is, rather surprisingly, what the definitive edition has become. But I have resisted the temptation on the quite solid ground that it would be grossly presumptuous on my part, since I am neither a textual critic nor a bibliographer, to pretend that I am in any way competent to defend those principles that now govern the preparation of the MLA-sponsored editions against those charges that have been leveled against them by Mr. Edmund Wilson and Mr. Lewis Mumford – though I cannot forgo mentioning with, I hope, pardonable pride that these principles are modeled almost entirely on those developed at the Ohio State University and the University of Virginia to govern the editorial preparation of our Centenary Edition of the Works of Nathaniel Hawthorne.

(Parenthetically, I do not believe that it ever occurred to the late William Charvat, to Roy Harvey Pearce, to Fredson Bowers, or to me, when we met in my office in 1963 to discuss for the first time the possibility of publishing a reliable edition of Hawthorne, that the edition proposed would ever become an issue of sufficiently wide concern to provoke, as it has, rather anxious telephone calls from such influential periodicals as *Time* and the *New York Review*.)

There is one thing, and one thing only, that I would like to say as publisher about the definitive edition as public issue. Mr. Wilson has made the point in his two articles in the *New York Review* on the MLA-sponsored editions that what are sorely needed in North America and throughout the world are convenient editions of our major authors; that is, physically compact, typographically pleasing, inexpensive, and – most important of all – reliable editions for the use of the student, his teacher, and the general reader. And this point is very well taken indeed. It must be said, however, that the Centenary Edition of the Works of Nathaniel Hawthorne has never been intended to answer this need. The hardcover Centenary Edition, as a definitive edition, provides the complete history of the transmission of the texts in the Hawthorne canon, and restores those texts, in the words of Fredson Bowers, to a form "as close ... in all details, to Hawthorne's final intentions as the preserved documents ... permit." It is obligatory, therefore, to supply all of the evidence on which the restoration of a given text is based.

That the lists of emendations and variants required to record fully the transmission of a Hawthorne text and to report completely the basis of its restoration and its claim to be definitive consume many pages, and that the bulk of this material does indeed produce large books, are not disputed. But it must be pointed out that the hardcover editions that Mr. Wilson finds so unwieldly were never intended for the use of students and teachers who must carry their books to class, or for the reader who turns to the classics during long flights on a jet.

Our original estimate of the number of copies of the Centenary Edition that we would sell altogether – that is, during the decade or more that will be required to prepare and to publish the ten to twelve volumes that will comprise it – was a modest one thousand copies. Clearly, we did not foresee a mass market for our wares. That the first four volumes of the Hawthorne Centenary Edition have sold in greater quantities than we have anticipated, and that we have gone into second and, in one case, even third printings, are, of course, gratifying; but the sales record to date has not exceeded the average number of copies that is expected for the usual specialized university-press book.

But though we have never considered the hardcover editions of the Centenary texts with their extensive apparatuses to be purely reading editions, we have attempted to serve the need for such editions by licensing commercial reprints of our texts, without the preliminary and appendix matter, in paperback or inexpensive hardcover form. To date, we have licensed reprint editions of Centenary texts to the Viking Press, the World Publishing Company, Harper and Row, the Bobbs-Merrill Company, W. W. Norton and Company, the Charles E. Merrill Company, and Scott, Foresman, and Company.

So much for the definitive edition as a public issue. I would like now to turn to the chief substance of my remarks: those general problems that have confronted us as the publisher of a multi-volume, definitive edition. I found, in the attempt to isolate and identify the general configurations of those difficulties we have encountered, some slight glow of satisfaction in the knowledge that our problems have become less knotty than they were when we began in 1964. I have immediately and automatically sought to counter this perhaps specious sense of well-being (in a superstitious but cautious regard for that principle of nemesis that seems often to work so vindictively in human affairs) with the silent warning to myself that this happy situation may not continue to obtain, that the problems that are peculiar to production of a definitive edition are multifarious and difficult to anticipate, and that routines carefully established and scrupulously observed may eventually prove inadequate to circumvent the pitfalls they are designed to avoid.

I think that I may explain in part how it is that – at the moment, at least – we seem, at the Ohio State University Press, to have dealt effectively with the major difficulties entailed by so large and demanding an undertaking, by describing very briefly the genesis of the Hawthorne project.

The project grew out of a conversation in which William Charvat expressed, rather forlornly, the wish that there could be made available to students of American literature reliable editions of the works of our foremost authors. A representative of the Ohio State University Press was bold enough to inquire what the Press, as a publisher in service to scholarship, might do to make such editions available. A wish somehow became a dream, then an idea, and finally a plan; and the Press, as co-instigator and co-developer of the plan, was active from the first in the formulation of the programme by which that plan was to be eventually implemented. We were fortunate, therefore, in avoiding those difficulties that so often confront the publisher who receives from an author or editor a manuscript that, no matter how soundly conceived and carefully prepared,

may have been executed largely in ignorance of those requirements that a publisher will impose on a manuscript offered him
for conversion to a book.

This early co-operation between editor and publisher was
made even more imperative by the kind of textual criticism our
edition was to be based upon. For this edition the initial step in
the editorial process was setting the copy-text in page proofs.
Simply because this step involves typographic design, typesetting, and production, it becomes also the first step in the
process of publication. The editing of the text of the crucial first
volume of the Centenary Edition, *The Scarlet Letter*, and publication of that text, began, therefore, at precisely the same time.
We thus became involved, at a primary stage, in the manuscript's preparation, and were able to shape that preparation to
our considerable advantage.

As a consequence, editors on the staff of the Press acquired
some knowledge of the basic principles of textual criticism; and
the general and textual editors of the Centenary Edition came
to learn the Press's house style and to understand the physical
requirements that are imposed on fair-copy manuscript for eco-
nomical, efficient, and expeditious typesetting – to some extent
becoming publisher's editors. (And I must interject at this point
that the complexities and intricacies of modern collating and
editorial techniques are quite capable, if not sufficiently dis-
couraged, of producing copy for publication that is a monument
to the ingenuity and dexterity of man in cutting and pasting
minute snippets of inscrutable holograph manuscript into complex montages that are uniquely and profoundly depressing to
any typesetter.) All are jointly concerned with the kind of
rigorous accuracy in transcription that is required of the definitive edition; and all are mercifully aware that such accuracy
needs to be imposed before copy has been typeset, and that
printers, less sensitive, perhaps, than they should be to the demands of scholarship, are inclined not to effect endless changes
in typeset matter at no cost whatsoever.

If by some necessary melding of the Press staff with the staff of the Center for Textual Studies of the Ohio State University, that agency whose function it is to prepare definitive texts for publication, we have had some measure of success in solving those problems that may occur when a publisher is not involved early enough in the planning for a major project, we cannot claim any very marked progress in remedying those difficulties that we have sometimes encountered when dealing with printers during the process of manufacture.

I should make it plain that the Ohio State University Press has no printing or manufacturing facilities of its own, and that we rely for manufacture of our books on the services of commercial firms. Over the years we have developed, with several well-known book-manufacturing companies, very cordial working relations, and have discovered, to our considerable delight, that those with which we have worked most closely have developed a remarkable sensitivity to the preferences of our editors in the division of words and other editorial niceties, and to the amount of letterspacing or carding our design and production people find tolerable.

It is distressing to report, therefore, that those printers who have understood us so well, and served us so well, when we have undertaken publication of titles whose demands do not exceed the limits of routine attention and normal practice have, on some occasions, been rendered oddly inefficient when confronted with the admittedly eccentric departures from routine that are imposed on production of a definitive edition.

I have already mentioned that the initial step in both the editorial preparation and the publication of a definitive edition is the setting in type, in pages, of the copy-text. For some reason, this not unreasonable requirement has produced grave consternation among some printers, who have seen our insistence that they typeset and compose into pages as much as one-half of a book, the other half of which is not yet written and cannot be

composed for another six months or a year, as placing an intoler-
able strain on the manufacturing process; they have been able
to persuade themselves to undertake the assignment at all – and
thereby to become party to the brutal violation of hallowed
routine and sacred procedure – only by assuming that some
impossibly arcane principle must guide and govern the publication of such books, a principle so rarified as to defy proper
identification and so impossible of explanation as to elude
common understanding. The unfortunate consequence of this
acquiescence in vice is that the printer thereby corrupted throws
his commonsense right out the window on the grounds that there
is nothing commonsensical about what it is that he is being
asked to do.

Printers bristle at any suggestion that one of their compositors
would knowingly set a typographical widow (by this term I refer
to the setting of a short line of text as the first line on a new text
page – a practice that is generally frowned upon); they are
incensed by any implication that one of their compositors could
be either so ignorant of accepted practice or so willful in his dis-
regard of it as to permit such an error, or that any proofreader
on their staffs would permit the abomination to survive beyond
that level at which house corrections are made; yet I have seen
such printers, in total abdication of their own competence as
craftsmen, proceed to deliver page proofs of a newly typeset
copy-text in which as many as ten consecutive pages open with
the forbidden short line.

I can only see a final solution to this problem in some exten-
sion to the printer of that process of education by which our
editors have been schooled in the easily apprehensible logic and
quite reasonable practice of textual criticism. We have achieved
some success in this direction after acknowledging that the fault
has lain somewhat with ourselves who have served unwittingly
to convey the idea that it is something recondite that controls the
exercises in which we invite our printers to play a part. In the

beginning we were at considerable pains to make clear to our printers that the copy-text is sacrosanct, that what seems peculiar or obsolete in substance, spelling, punctuation, or capitalization is precisely what must be preserved, and that much of the corruption of the Hawthorne canon during its long publishing history is directly attributable to the silent alterations effected by conscientious compositors of an earlier time, who violated authorial intention in the name of printing-house style or even of personal preference. However, more recently we have attempted to make it equally clear to our printers that although the apparent vagaries of the copy-text demand observance, the reconstruction of a reliable text does not entail complete abandonment of the time-honoured principles governing good composition in blind subservience to an elusive principle that dictates practice in incomprehensible ways.

If there was ever an impediment to that salutary learning process that has been imposed both upon our house editors and those textual specialists who are preparing the definitive edition for publication, it was – and then only very briefly – a tendency on the part of the editors of the text to resist the notion that the publisher's editors were capable of making any more than a purely mechanical contribution to the important work to which the textual staff had committed itself. There was, I think, a certain misgiving on the part of the textual editors that the result of the not too gentle ministrations of the publisher's editorial staff would be some violence done to the text so painstakingly established.

However, when our house editors proved themselves receptive to instruction by the textual editors, and showed themselves ready to aid the textual staff in acquiring the publishing skills that they so needed to have if editorial preparation and publication were to become a single process – as indeed they had to by virtue of the simultaneity with which they were to be carried out – then two groups of professional workers, who had shared only a vague but mutual distrust, became one, united in a single task and equipped with common skills.

I have made it clear, I hope, that it has not been my purpose here to defend the principles that have guided the editing of the works of Nathaniel Hawthorne, or the grounds on which this project and others like it have been undertaken, at great cost, by the universities that have seen fit to sponsor them. Yet I think that some clear idea of why the task at hand has been embarked upon is essential to all engaged in the project if their performance of often demanding duties is to be other than a sterile exercise in complexity; and I think that − simple-minded as it sounds − no solutions can be found to the problems posed by a project of such magnitude without this understanding.

Clearly, justification for what we have done must be found in what has been done for Hawthorne as author and for those critics who are his interpreters. If, in the Centenary Edition of *The Scarlet Letter*, Hester and Dimmesdale are not, in some previously suppressed but now restored authorial version of the final chapter, freed at last from the letters, *gules*, that burn their hearts, at least their tragic tale may now be read in the purity of its author's intention.

After studying Hawthorne in manuscript and the first-edition readings, the late William Charvat, a general editor of the Centenary Edition, was prompted to write to the textual editor, Professor Bowers:

It comes to me now, for the first time, that Hawthorne's style is essentially parenthetical, and that this characteristic reflects the basically essayistic, generalizing, and speculative quality of his fiction. His parentheses give him the latitude and flexibility that this quality requires. He modulates the degree of isolation of a unit by selecting ... just the right pair of separators: parentheses, or dashes, or commas. I don't think he did this selecting consciously, and probably the restoration of his own punctuation, after the compositors mangled it, looked like too much drudgery.

To an editor − to the one who establishes a clean text of a classic for responsible reprinting, or to the one shaping a new work for its initial appearance in print − to one committed, in short, to that search for "the right pair of separators" that will serve an author and his reader well, this testimony that what has been done by one professional charged with forming finally the work of another is of some consequence, is most welcome assurance indeed.

R. J. SCHOECK

TOWARDS A DEFINITION OF TERMS FOR
GROUP SCHOLARSHIP

NOT ALL SCHOLARS in the humanities have engaged in research and publication projects with their colleagues, and the proportions will vary from one period or field to another, even within the same discipline. Yet in some areas there seems to be a condescending attitude towards group projects – to use a generic term for co-operative, communal, and team scholarship (which I shall attempt to distinguish) – and some humanistic colleagues seem to feel that there is some kind of surrender involved in such participation, some cowardly following in the steps of the social or physical sciences. But, on the strength of my involvement in more than one such project, I would argue strongly – and I feel that the argument must be brought forward – that there are valuable gains accruing to the project itself, to the individual scholar, and to the parent institution. Besides, we humanists have in fact been at this kind of thing for some time. In a series of addresses given recently by David Knowles to the Royal Historical Society dealing with four great group projects,[1] we are given a view of such work. The first of the four was that of the learned Bollandists on the *Acta Sanctorum* and related publications; the second, that of the Maurists and their editions of the Fathers – both of these beginning in the seventeenth century, and the Bollandists still continuing, and both projects having published hundreds of texts, collections, and monographs. The third of Knowles' enterprises is the *Monumenta Germaniae Historica*, begun in the nineteenth century, reconstituted after the second world war and now active again; and the fourth, the Rolls Series, that astonishingly productive but amateur (and amateurish) English activity. Group projects in the humanities have had a distinguished history since the seventeenth century, long before they became the norm in the sciences.

In another context I have argued that there are certain kinds of problems which can be tackled only by teams; the alternatives are for individuals to be working too long or too far outside their competence in attempting to deal with really large, many-sided, and complex problems. Further, group scholarship is likely to spawn such valuable by-products as newsletters and journals, as was the case with the *MGH* and the development of its newsletter into the *Neues Archiv*, or with the Renaissance Society of America, whose newsletter first spun off the annual *Studies in the Renaissance* volume and then developed into the *Renaissance Quarterly*. Finally, there are important implications for graduate teaching in experiments with group scholarship, which I attempted to develop in March 1967 at York University in its conference on some of these problems. (The seminar is an important consideration here, and I shall return to it.)

Now let me move to suggest some definitions and discriminations of terminology. *Communal* would describe a project worked in common, that is, participated in jointly by a whole community. Exemplary of this would be the work of the Maurists, though it must be observed that even there the original

1 / Published as *Great Historical Enterprises* (London: Nelson, 1963).

conception of any project was that of an individual scholar, as was the responsibility for its execution: "When once a project had been approved and was under way, however, a scholar could draw upon his community [at the parish house of Saint-Germain-des-Prés], and even upon the whole [Benedictine] congregation, for assistance in copying manuscripts, reading proofs, indexing and the like ..."[2] It was for centuries, and may well still be, as Knowles claims, "the most impressive achievement of co-operative, or at least co-ordinated, scholarship in the modern world" – or, as I should urge, *communal* scholarship.

Co-operative is another necessary term, and the key is the sense of acting or co-operating jointly with others, for mutual benefit or common interest. One clear example, it seems to me, is the encyclopaedia, whether specialized, as with the *Social Sciences Encyclopedia* or the *New Catholic Encyclopedia*, or all-embracing, as with the *Encyclopaedia Britannica*. Yet even in these two, highly community-oriented, kinds of enterprise, the individual effort is not submerged: even the encyclopaedia will identify the individual contributor. We give witness also to the co-operative bibliography, of which one of the superlative productions in our times is the *PMLA* annual bibliography under the direction of Professor Harrison T. Meserole, in which some 125 scholars (all identified) labour together to produce a bibliography which for 1968 numbers approximately 22,000 items.

A third term is *team*: the root metaphor (so often lost sight of) is that of two or more horses harnessed to the same vehicle, for a common task. And teamwork is work carried out by two or more associates, all subordinating personal prominence or identification to the efficiency of the whole. With this term and concept, it seems to me that there is a vital turning, for in team scholarship the individual members are likely to lose a sense of the whole and to be dependent upon direction or management, whereas in the communal and co-operative forms of scholarship the effort of the individual may paradoxically be stronger. The

2 / *Ibid.*, p. 41.

ultimate of team writing is perhaps the production of a common style, as well as a common effort: witness *Time* magazine.

Group scholarship, then, remains a necessary term to include the different modes of procedure, but I urge distinctions like the three broad ones just suggested. To illustrate the point that there may be combinations of the three, I would offer the Yale Edition of St. Thomas More[3] as essentially a co-operative enterprise, with individual scholars or teams of scholars working on several volumes (as with Professors Hexter and Surtz on the *Utopia*, and more on the poems), but with a high degree of communal scholarly activity.

Group scholarship must also be related to parent organizations, where these are operative, and we should be firmly in command of such distinguishing terms as *institutes* and *centres* (recently discussed by L. K. Shook[4]), teaching schools and seminars. To turn to our earlier example, that of the Maurists, Knowles has made clear that their work was never "blueprinted and organized. There was nothing of the institute, the team or even the seminar, at Saint-Germain in the seventeenth century." But there was a larger sense of community and the Maurists' work, as I have suggested, mediated between the individual and the communal.

In North America – and here I protest in a short but necessary digression – too many things are called seminars. We have business pep-talks which are called seminars, and academic institutions which should know better too often use the term seminar for what ought more properly to be labelled conferences, colloquia, discussions, or simply small classes. The origins of the word *seminar* must be studied in the context of the nineteenth-century German university; the historian Ranke was one of the greatest academic teachers to develop what was already a traditional and rigorous academic structure: "He did

3 / Described in my introduction to *Editing Sixteenth-Century Texts* (Toronto: University of Toronto Press, 1966), pp. 7–10.

4 / Laurence K. Shook, CSB, "University Centers and Institutes of Medieval Studies," *Journal of Higher Education*, XXXVIII (December 1967), 484–92.

not indeed initiate, but he certainly canonized, the *Seminar*, a group of promising pupils to whom the master taught the skills of his craft in co-operative work with mutual help and rivalry in the field of his own studies."[5] Even a graduate course is not necessarily a seminar, and in North American graduate schools there are not enough seminars of the kind led by Ranke, in which the student aids the research of the master while learning technique, but also while working at a level that is beyond mere exercise and consequently more productive and meaningful. The attractions and advantages of a true seminar for a craft (or art, or mystery) like editing are obvious. Out of seminars may well come communal, or co-operative, or team scholarship, for much of such scholarship will be group generated.

Some reflections are perhaps in order, based largely on the experience of one successful group project at Yale, for I speak as one who values the contribution and co-operation and, still more, the friendship, of press editors – perhaps we are returning to something approaching Erasmus's even closer relations with his publisher-friends Aldus and Froben: he moved in and lived with his printer while a book was going through the press![6] First, to put it simply, a press editor ideally should be part of the university editorial community and a working member of the editorial committee of a project.[7] In the Yale experience there has been a great deal of the communication and the community life of scholarship: conferences, correspondence, contributions

5 / Knowles, *Great Historical Enterprises,* p. 41. I have discussed the root term *seminarium* in an article entitled "A Nursery of Correct and Useful Institutions" forthcoming in *Moreana* (1969). From this term comes the German *Seminar,* with the institution at Halle in 1696 of Francke's *Seminarium praeceptorum.* For a useful sketch of the history of *seminar/seminary* see the *New Catholic Encyclopedia,* s.v. *Seminar, History of.* There is some pointed discussion of seminars in Abraham Flexner, *Die Universitäten* (Berlin, 1932), pp. 200–1 (for Oxford), and 226–7 (for German universities).

6 / See P. S. Allen, "Erasmus' Relations with his Printers" in *Erasmus, Lectures and Wayfaring Sketches* (Oxford: Clarendon Press, 1934), pp. 118–23.

7 / In addition to this recommendation that a press editor be a member

to the work of others, participation in related works (often spun off from the central work), and so forth. For the projects involving group editing, which the twentieth-century is now attempting, development and perhaps even the initiation must come with the encouragement of larger academic structures – with "sympathy from the universities," to use Mr. Parker's phrase.

But that sympathy from the universities must be more than mere tolerance or verbal encouragement. The individual scholar and his research must be aided to the utmost that resources permit:

(a) by a centralizing of a common body of needed books, microfilms, or manuscripts, and tools of various kinds – at one place, presumably the central editorial office, with a bringing of involved scholars to that place;

(b) by recognition that scholars must travel to other libraries for work that cannot be done by correspondence or by consultation of microfilm or by like means – and if this be true of scholars at Yale, *a fortiori* it is true of scholars at less privileged institutions.

No contemporary university is simply a community of scholars any longer; at best, the university has become a galaxy of such communities. And, in the complex world of modern scholarship, many scholars will be members of, or will participate in, more than one community: allegiance becomes manifold. Yet these observed truths should not blind us to the fact that, in the humanities, where group projects are under way the essential problem is to provide means and structures for the work to proceed by mediating arrangements between the individual scholar and the larger group, by making available the ways and means and tools appropriate to the individual problem, and by providing the ideal environment for the task at hand.

----

of editorial committees, for parallel reasons one would also urge that a research librarian be a member of the advisory board of major editorial projects.

Proust and his Publishers

PHILIP KOLB

MARCEL PROUST'S relations with his publishers may be said to have followed in rather close parallel the history of his growing to maturity. In saying this, I am compelled to admit that the process appears to have taken an excessively long time. In all fairness, however, we should take into account the early age at which this author began his acquaintance with the publishing milieu. I do not of course mean to go back as far as the period when Proust helped to found and edit the privately printed periodical known as *Le Banquet*. He was then just twenty years old. But he was already writing some of the pieces that would be included in his first book, *Les Plaisirs et les jours*. So his first encounter with the publishing world was not far ahead.

As his publishers, Proust was to have one of the foremost houses of the nineteenth century, Calmann-Lévy, the editors of such giants as Stendhal, Renan, Loti, and Anatole France. As a matter of fact, it was probably the recommendation of Anatole France that persuaded Calmann-Lévy to accept Proust's book. Unfortunately for the young author, however, he enlisted too many patrons and collaborators for his own good. First he asked a society lady, Madame Madeleine Lemaire, to do the illustrations; then he had Reynaldo Hahn write music to accompany his poems; and, finally, he obtained the rare privilege of a preface signed by Anatole France himself, whose position was consecrated by election to the Académie française shortly before the book came out. This was all very well, but the book's appearance was amateurish, and its price prohibitive. At 13 francs 50, it was about ten francs too expensive for the average reader. This consideration was only to occur to Proust when it was too late; but he would in the future take every precaution to avoid that mistake when the time came to publish his novel.

Meanwhile, in his relations with Calmann-Lévy, he showed interest in such details as the choice and disposition of the illustrations. When the publication had been held up overlong by Mme Lemaire's delay in producing those drawings, Proust hounded the young editorial representative with whom he was dealing, a certain M. Hubert. He urged him to exert pressure on Mme Lemaire and suggested just how he might handle the situation. Finally, in desperation, he wrote to reproach him for having had the unfortunate idea of suggesting some new drawings for the book. Proust pointed out that the good lady had doubtless concluded "with feminine logic" that there was no hurry and, after having done one third of a drawing, had probably ordered models that would serve eventually, heaven knows when, for more sketches that she might get around to doing within a year or two. Proust asks: "Would you be so kind as to write her, and say this: 'Madam, our latest deadline is now past, if you do not send us *all* of the illustrations we shall not be able to get the book out this year ... ' "

On the other hand, we have a letter written in confidence by this same M. Hubert to Anatole France, when the book was in press, expressing his opinion of our young author. Reminding France of his promise to write a preface for the book, Hubert says that this is not the only favour France could do for their young friend. Hubert says he has already hinted to Proust that he might send his galley proofs to France. Hubert adds: "With the authority of your name, thanks to the confidence and the affection that he has in you and for you, the minor corrections or criticisms would be welcome and I won't hide the fact that I would consider them useful for the work whose sponsorship you are supposed to have accepted." He goes on to criticize Proust's work, specifying the lack of clarity or interest of certain essays, an abundance of naïve expressions, an awkward turn of phraseology, and a profusion of epithets, at times somewhat contradictory. He concedes that some of these blemishes lend a certain charm to the work, but complains that his attempts to suggest modifications have fallen on deaf ears.

That first book was ill conceived, as I have indicated, and ill fated. Twenty-two years after its publication the editors wrote to Proust to inform him that there remained in stock 1,171 out of the 1,500 copies of the original edition, and that they were obliged to dispose of the ones on hand for lack of space. Proust took the letter as a personal affront.

During the period when he was preparing his translations of Ruskin he came into contact with Gaston Calmette, editor of one of the great Paris newspapers of the time, the *Figaro*. Calmette did not particularly appreciate what Proust wrote, but he did accept his articles from time to time, occasionally even commissioning him to do them. It was the *Figaro* that published a series on Paris society, and later the brilliant pastiches on the theme of the Lemoine affair, parodying famous writers. Proust felt himself under obligations, and knowing the editor's taste for hobnobbing with aristocrats, he would on occasion give an elegant dinner in his honour. Calmette very nearly made a name for himself in literary history by proposing to publish Proust's novel in serial form several years before it actually came out. Agreement was reached for its publication, and Proust sent his manuscript at the appointed time. But he was so unaccustomed to the ways of the world that, instead of addressing the package to the editor, he sent it instead to one of the literary critics on Calmette's staff.[1] In so doing he offended the editor's susceptibilities by seeming to consider his literary judgment less sure than that of his subordinate. Calmette smouldered, and nothing further was heard from him until about six months later, when the humbled novelist went to recover his unwanted manuscript.

When, in the summer of 1909, Proust had first consulted Calmette about a publisher for his novel, he actually had written only the rough draft of the beginning and the end of the novel. The remainder of it was outlined mostly in his head. It was nearly three years later before he had written it all out, and had a typescript of the first 700 pages. At this point he asked his friend Mme Genevieve Straus to approach Calmette about finding an editor. Calmette spoke to Fasquelle and obtained his agreement to publish the novel. Meanwhile, Proust wrote to Gaston Gallimard, the head of a new publishing house called *La Nouvelle Revue française*, asking whether he would consider the novel. Thus Proust submitted two typescripts simultaneously to two different firms, admitting to the second that the novel had already been accepted by the first. If his manner of dealing with two publishers at once was irregular, the publishers themselves dealt with Proust in a way that was not exactly above reproach. Fasquelle had been imprudent enough to promise to publish the novel without having seen it. He thereupon gave Proust's bulky typescript – 733 pages – to a reader. And that particular reader – a fact that I reveal here for the first time – happened to be someone whom Proust had met when as a young man he frequented Mme Lemaire's salon, and with whom he seems to have exchanged mutual feelings approaching disdain and hostility. Evidence of this I see in the way Proust pokes fun at the poetry of the man in question in one of his satirical pieces in *Les Plaisirs et les jours*. In any case, the report on Proust's novel which was

1 / André Beaunier, whose reputation as a critic and novelist was well established, whereas Calmette was known only as an administrator and a journalist.

submitted to Fasquelle by the elder man is an interesting docu-
ment. But its discoverer, Henri Bonnet, identifies the man only
as a poet named Jacques Madeleine, failing to note that he was
better known at the time as Jacques Normand (1848–1931),
and that he frequented several of the same salons as did Proust.[2]
The contents of the report amount to a venomous harangue
against the latter's novel, in which personal hostility toward the
novelist is scarcely veiled. The upshot is that Fasquelle retracted
his promise to publish the novel. He did so just a short time after
Proust had received word of its rejection by *La Nouvelle Revue
française*.

It is well known that that second rejection was almost entirely
the result of a negative decision by André Gide. Later Gide
testified that he had done no more than leaf through the typescript and glance at two or three of its pages. He confessed that
he had acted under the impression that Proust was an amateur
of a sort he wanted to keep out of his group. Proust had inad-
vertently confirmed this impression by offering to pay for the
edition, and by saying that his book was dedicated to the editor
of the *Figaro*. So there again, as with Fasquelle's reader, it was
a question of prejudice instead of an impartial judgment of the
work submitted.

The novel was forthwith submitted to the firm of Ollendorff,
with strong supporting recommendations from two prominent
writers, Edmond Rostand and Louis de Robert. But again it was
turned down. Proust, fearing he might not live to correct the
proof if things continued at such a rate, determined to have the
novel published forthwith at his own expense. Bernard Grasset
agreed to do the work; Proust was to pay 1,750 francs ($350)
for the edition; the volume was to cost 3 francs 50 ($.70) of
which Proust was to receive 1 franc 50 ($.30) in royalties.

2 / Henri Bonnet, *Le Figaro littéraire*, 8 December 1966, p. 15. Cf. *Qui
êtes-vous? Annuaire des contemporains* (Paris: Ch. Delagrave, 1908),
p. 366; A. de Fouquières, *Mon Paris et ses parisiens* (Paris: Pierre Horay,
1953), I, pp. 179–80.

Within about a month of signing the contract with Grasset, he had received his first set of proof. If we take a look at the author at this point in his career, we find him disconcertingly unfamiliar with matters pertaining to the production of books. He did not even know some of the commonest terminology of the printing press, such as "bon à tirer," the French expression for "OK to print." Instead of correcting the galleys, he rewrote so much of the original text that there remained scarcely one out of every twenty lines. As Proust himself admits, he had written "a new book" on proof sheets. He thought of offering Grasset an indemnity, but before he could do so, Grasset had remonstrated, sending him a bill for an additional 595 francs ($120). By the time Proust had corrected several sets of proof he had lost sixty pounds in weight, and had become so thin that he was hardly recognizable. Despite all this work, when the book came out, in November 1913, it was replete with typographical errors. According to Gabriel Astruc, who marked the errors in his copy, they came to a total of nearly one thousand. Proust had never learned how to do a proper job of proof reading. Trouble with his eyes from about 1917 until his death made the task increasingly difficult, and he finally had to rely entirely on his publishers to do the proof reading for him, so that he might concentrate on the completion of his novel.

Today we know how Gide and his group, as soon as they read *Du Côté de chez Swann* in print, realized what a mistake they had made in rejecting it. They immediately offered to take charge of the remaining volumes of the novel. Proust was eager to accept the offer to migrate to the *NRF*, but he declined for fear of hurting Grasset's feelings. Only the first volume had been published when war broke out in August 1914 and literary publications were suspended. But nearly two years were to pass before Proust wrote to Grasset, then in Switzerland, about rescinding their contract, so that publication of the remaining portions of the novel could be undertaken by the *NRF*. Another year went by before proof began coming again, and yet another before printing of the second volume was completed, just after the signing of the Armistice. That volume, *A l'ombre des jeunes filles en fleurs*, did not appear on the book stands, however, until seven more months, along with a volume of Proust's collected parodies and other articles. The reason for mentioning such delays is that they had serious implications for an author who knew his days were numbered, and who had so much work yet to accomplish.

The man with whom he had to deal as head of the publishing firm, Gaston Gallimard, although devoted to Proust, appears from his correspondence with him to have been somewhat less concerned with literature than with business and his own personal affairs. In one lively dispute, Proust accuses him of playing on words when he says he is "an editor, not a printer"; Proust claims the edition of *A l'ombre des jeunes filles en fleurs* had been "sabotaged." Nevertheless he adroitly managed to strike a happy balance between protestations of friendship and an insistence on his rights. He showed slight interest in money matters, but kept a close watch on questions of printing, publicity, and translations. His sole objective was to win new readers for his novel.

The person who did the most to maintain good relations and avoid misunderstandings was Jacques Rivière, who, after the war, had taken over the editorship of Gide's periodical, the *NRF*, and made of it the most important literary journal of the period. A critic of considerable stature, Rivière was among the first to understand the significance of the innovation that Proust's novel brought to French literature. Rivière himself was in poor health from having been wounded and kept a prisoner during most of the war. He also was beset with financial difficulties and worries about his wife and children. Yet he gave selflessly of his time and energies, writing and lecturing to enhance Proust's reputation and to bring him a wider public. It was he who "discovered" Proust as a critic, and persuaded him to write the articles on Flaubert and Baudelaire. At Proust's death, he gathered an impressive number of articles in hommage to the novelist which he published in a special issue of the *NRF*. And during the couple of years he had yet to live, Rivière and his wife helped decipher the posthumous portions of Proust's novel and to prepare them for publication. Rivière has given us a rare example of devotion to an ideal.

If Proust was indeed slow in maturing, in a certain sense, as we indicated earlier, he did unquestionably overcome his childish, snobbish traits to become a man of real stature. Assuredly he must have been thinking of himself when in his novel he showed Elstir to have shed his earlier incarnation of M. Biche to become a man of wisdom.[3] Proust's correspondence in his later years impresses us not only for the ease and distinction of his style, but also for his ability to dash letters off in all directions while at the same time feverishly completing his novel. We can see too in what a masterful manner he dealt with publishers and men of letters. He was diplomatic but firm. The ones we cannot help pity are his printers. In one of his letters he complains of the deplorable chaos of some proof sheets he has just received. But if we examine his manuscripts we are apt to wonder how the printers managed to make anything at all out of them. Probably no author since Balzac has tried the capacities of his printers and the patience of his publishers more severely than did Marcel Proust.

3 / *A l'ombre des jeunes filles en fleurs*, ed. P. Clarac and A. Ferré (Paris: Gallimard, 1954, Pléiade edition), I, pp. 863–64.

Maxwell Perkins:
The Editor as Critic

A. WALTON LITZ

Founded in 1846, the publishing house of Charles Scribner's Sons is one of the oldest and most distinguished in America. The current president, Charles Scribner, Jr., is the sixth member of the family to hold that office, and this continuity in ownership has been largely responsible for the firm's long-standing reputation as a house which maintains the highest standards in editing and production. Family ownership has also led to a meticulous concern with the firm's history, and the Scribner archives recently deposited in the Princeton University Library provide invaluable evidence of the changing relations between author and publisher over the past century.[1] Virtually complete to the centennial year of 1946, the letterbooks, business records, and "office histories" are so methodically organized and indexed that they yield a running commentary on the economic and editorial practices of American publishing. Of even greater

1 / Material from the Scribner archives is published by permission of Charles Scribner's Sons, and is protected by copyright. Thomas Wolfe's "Note for the Publisher's Reader" is published by permission of the Estate of Thomas Wolfe.

interest to scholars and critics will be the files of authors' correspondence: the firm's connections with its authors were usually long and often personal, and some of the files on individual authors are extraordinarily rich in literary value. The Edith Wharton collection, for example, contains well over 700 letters from her, along with corrected galleys and a vast amount of publisher's correspondence; the Galsworthy collection, with nearly 2,500 letters, provides a full bibliographical and financial record of his American publications, as well as a great deal of biographical information.

As might be expected, the Scribner archives are richest in those authors who were fortunate enough to have Maxwell Perkins as their editor. The Fitzgerald collection contains nearly 500 letters from the author, mostly to Perkins, and over 1,200 related documents – carbon replies, financial records, letters to agents and other publishers. The Thomas Wolfe collection forms a complete record of the intricate negotiations between Wolfe and his Scribner editors, while the Hemingway collection – currently restricted in access – is equally impressive in its range and literary interest. Some of this material has already been used in recent studies of Fitzgerald, Wolfe, and Hemingway, but it will be many years before all the important documents are identified and assimilated. All I can hope to accomplish in this paper is to provide a few notes on Perkins's editorial methods, and to suggest the ways in which his work was symptomatic of a general departure from the traditional relationship of author, editor, and publisher.

Born in 1884, Maxwell Perkins graduated from Harvard in 1907 and worked for a while as a reporter on the New York *Times*. In the spring of 1910 he entered the advertising department of Scribners and in 1914 was transferred to the editorial staff. One of his last acts before entering the editorial department was to write to his old school and college friend, Van Wyck Brooks, informing Brooks that the manuscript of *America's Coming-of-Age* had been rejected by the senior editor at Scribners, William Crary Brownell. Brownell had acknowledged that Brooks was a "live wire," but he objected to the way in which Brooks swept America's genteel writers "into the dustbin of the past with a contemptuousness of gesture which was at least pre-mature."[2] Perkins reacted quite mildly to Brownell's decision, merely promising that he would pass the manuscript on to another publisher, but he must have known that his own future as a Scribners editor would depend in large measure upon his success in changing the firm's conservative and genteel values. Like Van Wyck Brooks, he would have to introduce a new view of the literary tradition. The Scribners of 1914 was a prosperous and highly regarded publishing house, famous for its scholarly and religious publications, and with a strong literary list that included Henry James, Galsworthy, and Edith Wharton. Nonetheless, the firm had resisted many of the forms and subjects of contemporary fiction. A novel by Hamlin Garland had been declined "on the ground that it contained slang, profanity, vulgarity, agnosticisms, and radicalism."[3] Stephen Crane's *Maggie* and George Moore's *Esther Waters* had been refused, along with Arnold Bennett's *Old Wives' Tale*. Charles Scribner was not insensitive to the power of these works, but he felt that their publication would damage the firm's reputation and break faith with its genteel readers. In a letter to his London agent, L. W. Bangs, Scribner acknowledged that *The Old Wives' Tale* was "skillfully done," but he balked at a story which was "a decidedly unpleasant one with two streams of narrative both leading to divorces and with unpleasant and sordid details."[4] Later Scribner wrote candidly to Bangs of the firm's dilemma:

2 / *Editor to Author: The Letters of Maxwell E. Perkins*, ed. John Hall Wheelock (New York, 1950), p. 10.

3 / Charles A. Madison, *Book Publishing in America* (New York, 1966), p. 94. For an excellent account of conservative policy at Scribners, see pp. 89–95 and 196–207 of Madison's study.

4 / Scribner archives, letterbook cs–b #5; Charles Scribner to L. W. Bangs, 19 July 1906.

... so many of the well-known English authors – like Wells, Arnold Bennett, George Moore, and others – are too free and coarse in their handling of delicate questions, to suit us. I enjoy their books personally but our imprint would sometimes be injured by association with such books. It is very hard to tell where the dividing line comes and we sometimes make mistakes, for the public is becoming more and more callous.[5]

One key to Perkins's eventual success as an editor lay in his ability to convince the firm that greater freedom would not injure "the imprint." This matter strikes much deeper than contemporary issues of propriety and "good taste," since in his reactions against editorial timidity Perkins revealed that liberal attitude toward artistic expression which enabled him to understand and guide the authors of a new generation. His objections to unofficial censorship had nothing to do with literary fashion, but were founded on a broad view of the publisher's responsibility to society. Late in his career Perkins summed up his creed in a brilliant critique of the publisher who seeks to impose his own values on the public.

If he is that kind of man, let him speak for himself and be a writer. But the function of a publisher in society is to furnish a means by which anyone of a certain level of intelligence and abilities can express his views. A publisher should not be, as such, a partisan, however strongly partisan he may be as an individual. If he allows his partisanship to govern him in his choice of books, he is a traitor to the public. He is supposed to furnish a forum for the free play of the intellect, in so far as he possibly can. That is the whole American theory – that opinions can be given a means of full expression, and that the public, hearing all of them and considering them, will eventually approximate a right conclusion. Every profession has its own particular code of ethics, its own morality, that its members must adhere to or they betray it. And a primary element in the

5 / Scribner archives, letterbook CS–B #6; Charles Scribner to L.W. Bangs, 8 February 1911.

morality of the publisher is that he shall not let his own personal views obstruct the way for the expression of counter-views.[6]

Time and again in his career as an editor Perkins put these brave generalities into practice. He was firmly convinced that open expression was the only means of countering the prurient imagination, and in his frequent replies to irate readers he defended the essential morality of the artist.

As to censorship of literature, while I must agree that there are sometimes books which are deliberately contrived to appeal to vicious instincts, I believe that freedom of speech is the very basis of this nation, and that what damage, if any, may come from such books should be risked because of the much greater damage that would come if the principles of censorship were introduced and progressed ... I have read the opinions of various people of high repute, in the *Journal American* "Crusade" against salacious or obscene books, and most of them seem to me to have no understanding of literature at all.[7]

Perkins was by inheritance a New Englander with a puritanical cast of mind, and he was often troubled personally by the language of the new fiction (especially the dialogue in Hemingway's *A Farewell to Arms*); yet he was determined "to play the game to the limit,"[8] as he said in a letter to Hemingway, and he recognized the honesty of Hemingway's style. He understood immediately that *The Sun Also Rises*, in spite of its frank details, was "a healthy book with marked satirical implications upon novels which are not. – Sentimentalized, subjective novels, marked by sloppy, hazy thought."[9] Like Harriet Weaver, the austere Quaker publisher of Joyce and Eliot, Perkins went beyond the imperatives of current literary fashion and based his

6 / *Editor to Author*, pp. 244–45; letter of 25 May 1944.

7 / *Editor to Author*, pp. 280–81; Letter of 27 September 1946.

8 / Scribner archives; Maxwell Perkins to Ernest Hemingway, 12 July 1929.

9 / Scribner archives; Maxwell Perkins to Ernest Hemingway, 20 July 1926.

editorial creed on the broad principles of social democracy. It was this open-minded and tolerant attitude which made him the ideal adviser to writers of the post-war generation.

But although Perkins's essential liberalism was the key to his personal success as an editor, his critical ability was the foundation of his technical success. When, in Malcolm Cowley's words, the house of Scribner "took a sudden leap from the age of innocence into the middle of the lost generation,"[10] it was Perkins's taste and literary tact which kept the firm from landing on its face. Born in the decade that produced the first great generation of twentieth-century writers, and educated at the Harvard of Wallace Stevens and T. S. Eliot, Perkins found that he shared with his young authors a sense of their place in time and a new attitude toward literary value and form. His initial reactions to the works of young writers were as acute and precise as those of the best contemporary critics. His instant recognition of Fitzgerald's talent, even in the awkward early version of *This Side of Paradise*, is the most celebrated of Perkins's discoveries, but the correspondence in the Scribner archives is filled with similar instances of his instinct for quality. When Fitzgerald suggested that he read Hemingway's early stories, Perkins responded with this quick estimate:

As for Hemingway: I finally got his "In our time" which accumulates a fearful effect through a series of brief episodes, presented with economy, strength and vitality. A remarkable, tight, complete expression of the *scene*, in our time, as it looks to Hemingway.[11]

In contrast to the many editors who rejected Hemingway's stories as mere anecdotes or sketches, Perkins seized immediately on their essential strengths. The same critical awareness is evident in his initial reaction to the chaotic manuscript of Thomas Wolfe's "O Lost" (later *Look Homeward, Angel*). From the

10 / Malcolm Cowley, "Unshaken Friend: II" (part II of a two-part profile), *The New Yorker*, xx (8 April 1944), 30.
11 / Scribner archives, box 51, folder 9; Maxwell Perkins to F. Scott Fitzgerald, 24 February 1925.

moment he read the first scene, where Oliver W. Gant and his brother stand by the roadside and watch a division of Lee's Army marching toward Gettysburg, Perkins knew that there was a book to be extricated and published.[12]

It is important to understand that Perkins's gift was critical, not "creative" in the usual sense of that word. "The trouble with most editors is that they are disappointed authors," he once remarked. "The source of a book must be the author. You can only help the author to produce what he has in his compass."[13] Perkins never tried to impose his vision upon a manuscript; instead, he sought first to obtain a precise sense of the author's intention, the basic design, and then if help was needed he would guide the author toward fulfilment of that design. When the author was disciplined and self-assured, as with Hemingway, Perkins had the good sense to leave him alone. In his letters to Hemingway concerning *A Farewell to Arms* Perkins displayed a fine understanding of the novel's structure and themes, but he carefully restricted his comments to a few tentative suggestions.

I have thought and talked about it for some three month now, and beyond the few slight comments on the margin of the proof I have one or two more serious ideas on it which I dare give you because I know you will know easily whether to reject them, and won't mind doing it ...

The first point relates to the combination of the two elements of the book, – Love and War. They combine, to my mind, perfectly up to the point where Catherine and Lieutenant Henry get to Switzerland; – thereafter, the war is almost forgotten by them and by the reader, – though not quite. And psychologically it should be all but forgotten; – it would be by people so profoundly in love, and so I do not think what I at first thought, that you might bring more

12 /For Perkins's reminiscences of his first encounter with Wolfe's manuscript, see his article on "Thomas Wolfe," *Harvard Library Bulletin*, 1 (Autumn 1947), 269–77.

13 / Malcolm Cowley, "Unshaken Friend: 1," *The New Yorker*, xx (1 April 1944), 34.

news of it or remembrances of it into this part. Still, I can't shake off the feeling that War, which has deeply conditioned this love story – and does so still passively – should still do so actively and decisively. It would if Catherine's death might probably not have occurred except for it ... and if the doctor said so during that awful night, in just a casual sentence, the whole story would turn back upon War in the realization of Henry and the reader.

I say this with the realization that a man in this work may make a principle into an obsession, as professors do. Unity? Nothing is so detestable as the *neat* ending. But Catherine was in a physical condition which made her unable to come through the Caesarian ... If it is true that the War produced that condition, I don't think it would make the conclusion *artificial*, or too *neat* if it were said, or implied. Of course in a deeper sense the reader does feel that War permeated the entire thing. – I can argue either way but even that fact makes the question worth raising ...

The other point regards the intense pain of the hospital episode. It's physical painfulness is such as by itself – apart from all the rest of the story – to completely absorb the reader, and this may not be right. You might lessen it by reducing the physical detail, perhaps.[14]

There is no indication that Hemingway followed Perkins's suggestions while recasting the ending of the novel: he did eliminate a few paragraphs which, at the close of the original version, outlined the fates of the novel's survivors, but the connections between War and Love remained implicit and the details of Catherine's death were retained in all their painful exactitude. Perkins's intelligent and tactful advice did, however, establish his credentials as a trustworthy critic. In an interview given after Perkins's death in 1947, Hemingway paid tribute to his editor as someone who "never asked me to change anything I wrote except to remove certain words which were not then publishable. Blanks were left, and anyone who knew the words would

14 / Scribner archives; Maxwell Perkins to Ernest Hemingway, 24 May 1929.

know what they were. For me he was not an editor. He was a wise friend and wonderful companion."[15]

The long relationship between Perkins and Fitzgerald was also that of "friend and companion." After Fitzgerald's death, when Perkins was collecting letters for the centenary history of Scribners, he was amazed to discover how much of his discussion with Fitzgerald had been carried on by mail. So close had their relationship been that he remembered most of the contents of the letters as "conversation."[16] Unlike Hemingway, Fitzgerald often had need of editorial encouragement and guidance, and as his control over his art weakened the advice of Perkins took on much greater significance. The painful search for an adequate form in *Tender Is the Night* has been recorded in detail by M. J. Bruccoli,[17] and the Scribner archives provide ample evidence of Perkins's involvement in this process; but as early as the making of *The Great Gatsby* (1924–25) Perkins's critical judgment played a major role. Like Ezra Pound's suggested revisions to *The Waste Land*, Perkins's comments on the manuscript of *The Great Gatsby* were detailed and practical, designed to fix Fitzgerald's attention on the basic design of the novel. Perkins was unstinting in his praise of the work's "*glamour*," seeing it as "a marvelous fusion, into a unity of presentation, of the extraordinary incongruities of life today."[18] His criticisms were directed at specific weaknesses: Gatsby's vagueness, the inadequate treatment of his business affairs, occasional inconsistencies in narrative method. Perkins and Fitzgerald obviously shared the same vision of the finished novel, and as the title fluctuated among a half-dozen alternatives they worked together

15 / Madison, *Book Publishing in America*, p. 210.

16 / Scribner archives, box 53, folder 32; Maxwell Perkins to Mrs. Samuel J. Lanahan, 19 April 1945.

17 / *The Composition of "Tender Is the Night": A Study of the Manuscripts* (Pittsburgh, 1963).

18 / Scribner archives, box 51, folder 8; Maxwell Perkins to F. Scott Fitzgerald, 18 November 1924. See also *Editor to Author*, pp. 38–41.

to sharpen the narrative focus.[19] Fitzgerald was encouraged to find that his "favorite spots in the book" were also Perkins's favorites, and he gave close attention to his editor's "excellent and most helpful" suggestions.[20] No better example can be found of Perkins's editorial skill: by grasping immediately what he called the "point of observation," and by recognizing the aims of Fitzgerald's irony, he was able to offer detailed criticism without jeopardizing in any way the integrity of the author's work.

The cases discussed so far have not been unusual examples of editorial activity, although Perkins clearly operated with greater sensitivity and authority than most editors can muster. It was his association with Thomas Wolfe that gave Perkins the reputation of a "creative" editor, a reputation he never sought and firmly rejected. The well-known complexities of Wolfe's sprawling manuscripts, as recounted and exaggerated in literary gossip; the generous dedication which Wolfe affixed to *Of Time and the River* ("To Maxwell Evarts Perkins, a great editor and a brave and honest man ... a work to be known as *Of Time and the River* is dedicated with the hope that all of it may be in some way worthy of the loyal devotion and the patient care which a dauntless and unshaken friend has given to each part of it, and without which none of it could have been written"); the frank revelations in Wolfe's *Story of a Novel* – all these combined to promote the myth of Perkins as manipulator and co-author. *Publishers' Weekly*, in a tribute called "Laurels to an Editor," spoke of Perkins as if he were the manager of an irresponsible and somewhat punchdrunk prize-fighter, while Bernard DeVoto wrote slightingly of novels put together by "Mr. Perkins and the

19 / In addition to *Gatsby* and *The Great Gatsby*, Fitzgerald considered at one time or another the following titles: "On the Road to West Egg," "Gold-hatted Gatsby," "The High-bouncing Lover," "Among the Ash Heaps and Millionaires," "Trimalchio in West Egg."

20 / *The Letters of F. Scott Fitzgerald*, ed. Andrew Turnbull (New York, 1963), p. 170.

assembly-line at Scribner's."[21] Comments such as these were at least partly responsible for Wolfe's decision to leave Scribners after the publication of his first two novels, and the legend of Perkins as writer-editor has persisted to this day.

There is ample evidence of the working relationship which developed between Wolfe and Perkins.[22] The huge manuscripts were radically cut, large sections of narrative being either eliminated or transposed. Purple passages were reduced in size and, although Wolfe's words were seldom changed, the tone of his work was altered at many points. This process of organization and condensation is well known; what has been less clear to readers and critics is the extent to which these changes clarified or distorted Wolfe's basic design. The Scribner archives shed a good deal of light on this problem, and help us to understand the great attraction that Perkins felt for Wolfe's fiction. The cast of Perkins's mind, and the flexibility of his editorial methods, are nowhere better displayed than in his work on *Look Homeward, Angel* and *Of Time and the River*.

Perkins saw from the first what Wolfe was trying to do. He was fascinated by Wolfe's desire to record the peculiar colours and contours of American life, and he could forgive Wolfe almost anything because of this feeling for a national experience which Perkins and Wolfe, each in his own way, had inherited and shared. He agreed with Wolfe that the characters in his fiction were "*great* people and that they should be told about."[23]

---

21 / *Publishers' Weekly* (23 March 1935), 1230–31; Bernard DeVoto, "Genius is not Enough," *Forays and Rebuttals* (Boston, 1936), p. 331.

22 / See, for example, the two recent biographies by Elizabeth Nowell (New York, 1960) and Andrew Turnbull (New York, 1967), as well as Wolfe's own *The Story of a Novel* (New York, 1936) and Perkins's two memoirs: "Scribner's and Tom Wolfe," *Carolina Magazine*, XLVIII (October 1938) and "Thomas Wolfe," *Harvard Library Bulletin* (see note 12). The revisions of the novels are discussed in great detail in Francis E. Skipp's unpublished PH.D. dissertation, "Thomas Wolfe and His Scribner's Editors" (Duke University, 1962). Skipp's intelligent and sensible conclusions are strongly supported by material in the Scribner archives.

23 / Maxwell Perkins, "Thomas Wolfe," *Harvard Library Bulletin*, 272.

The problem was that of finding a governing form, and in his search for this form Perkins discovered two unsettling things: Wolfe's entire artistic impulse was expansive, centrifugal, and his fiction was *literally* autobiographical. This author who once walked through the streets proudly chanting "I wrote ten thousand words today – I wrote ten thousand words today" was not, Perkins realized, constructing the conventional *Bildungsroman*:

I remember the horror with which I realized, when working with Thomas Wolfe on his manuscript of "The Angel," that all these people were almost completely real, that the book was literally autobiographical. I had thought that it was only so in the way that "David Copperfield" was, or Thackeray's "Pendennis." Tom saw how I felt, from my expression, I suppose, and he said, "But you don't understand. I think that they are great people." He meant his mother and father, and so on. Anyhow, the book was a great book, and there wasn't anything to be done about it, but it did give great pain for a time.[24]

It is a sign of Perkins's editorial genius that he could shift from the academic, almost Flaubertian standards he used in criticizing the well-made fiction of Fitzgerald or Hemingway and adjust to the brawling world of Wolfe's creation.

Faced with all the problems that stemmed from Wolfe's total involvement in his subject-matter, Perkins sought for an organizing principle and found it in the memories and thoughts of Eugene Gant: Eugene would be the focus of everything. As he trimmed and transposed to fit this principle, Perkins was pleased to discover that all his suggestions were ones that Wolfe could easily see, or had already seen.[25] In effect, Perkins followed a pattern which Wolfe had already visualized but was unable to achieve alone because of his inability to disengage himself from his subject. When the manuscript of *Look Homeward,*

24 / *Ibid.*, pp. 271–72, 276; *Editor to Author*, p. 296.
25 / Maxwell Perkins, "Scribner's and Tom Wolfe," in *The Enigma of Thomas Wolfe*, ed. Richard Walser (Cambridge, Mass., 1953), p. 59.

Angel (then called "O Lost") arrived at Scribners it was accompanied by the extraordinary "Note for the Publisher's Reader" which is printed as an appendix to this paper. With its detailed self-analysis and touching belief in the importance of what he had done, this "Note" reveals Wolfe's deep conviction that his work possessed an organic form which could triumph over his obsessions with language and self-revelation. In fact, the "Note" shows Wolfe's complete awareness of those defects in the novel's proportions that would have to be countered in the process of revision. The same ability at self-criticism is reflected in Wolfe's pocket notebook of the time; before his second conference with Perkins he jotted down a series of detailed suggestions for revision and cutting.[26] It seems clear that Perkins did not work against the grain of Wolfe's talent: instead he accomplished with Wolfe's co-operation what neither could have accomplished alone, a refashioning of the novel's surface which liberated the natural pattern. As always, his specific suggestions were based on a firm critical grasp of the work's essential strengths. It was this sense of general form which led Perkins to request that the sections of Wolfe's second novel be given to him as they were written, so he could follow the emerging form: "when we begin to get the book ready for the printer," he wrote to Wolfe, "you will probably want me also to understand it fully, all round."[27]

When Maxwell Perkins's career is compared with that of his predecessors in the editorial department at Scribners, or with the career of the typical reader in a nineteenth-century publishing house, we are struck by radical differences, both in editorial methods and in the editor's personal relationship with his authors. Friendship and sound advice had always flowed from editor to author, but I can think of few previous editors who became — strictly in their editorial roles — equally important

26 / Elizabeth Nowell, *Thomas Wolfe: A Biography* (New York, 1960), pp. 133–34. One section of the notes was headed "Proposal for Condensation."

27 / Scribner archives, box 171, folder 4; Maxwell Perkins to Thomas Wolfe, 9 August 1933.

figures in the literary life of their times. It is difficult to generalize upon the reasons for this change, since they reflect larger changes in the structure of the literary establishment and perhaps in the nature of literature itself. One possibility is a shift in the social relationship between author and publishing house which opened the way for a freer exchange between author and editor. Another cause might be changes in the economic structure of the publishing house which placed the editor not in the traditional position of "reader," but in a new position as someone who deals with the entire range of an author's literary and financial problems. One thinks also of the increasing size and complexity of publishing, bringing in the age of the specialized editor who usurps some of the functions once exercised by the president or the director. Another shift, most problematic of all, might be inferred from the peculiar characteristics of modern literature. If, as Paul Valéry once observed in a remark which would seem to hold true for many authors of this century, a work of art is never finished, only abandoned, where better to abandon it than on the desk of a sympathetic and talented editor. But whatever the reasons for his special prestige may have been, Maxwell Perkins stands with Sylvia Beach, Harriet Weaver, and John Quinn as one of those catalytic figures who emerged with the great generation of twentieth-century writers and, by combining personal and financial support with perceptive criticism, became an essential part of the literary history of their age.

NOTE FOR THE PUBLISHER'S READER

This book, by my estimate, is from 250,000 to 280,000 words long. A book of this length from an unknown writer no doubt is rashly experimental, and shows his ignorance of the mechanics of publishing. That is true: this is my first book.

But I believe it would be unfair to assume that because this is a very long book it is too long a book. A revision would, I think, shorten it somewhat. But I do not believe any amount of revision would make it a short book. It could be shortened by scenes, by pages, by thousands of words. But it could not be shortened by half, or a third, or a quarter.

There are some pages here which were compelled by a need for fullness of expression, and which had importance when the book was written not because they made part of its essential substance, but because, by setting them forth, the mind was released for its basic work of creation. These pages have done their work of catharsis, and may now be excised. But their excision would not make a short book.

It does not seem to me that the book is overwritten. Whatever comes out of it must come out block by block and not sentence by sentence. Generally, I do not believe the writing to be wordy, prolix, or redundant. And separate scenes are told with as much brevity and economy as possible. But the book covers the life of a large family intensively for a period of twenty years, and in rapid summary for fifty years. And the book tries to describe not only the visible outer lives of all these people, but even more their buried lives.

The book may be lacking in plot but it is not lacking in plan. The plan is rigid and densely woven. There are two essential movements – one outward and one downward. The outward movement describes the effort of a child, a boy, and a youth for release, freedom, and loneliness in new lands. The movement of experience is duplicated by a series of widening concentric circles, three of which are represented by the three parts of the book. The downward movement is represented by a constant excavation into the buried life of a group of people, and describes the cyclic curve of a family's life – genesis, union, decay, and dissolution.

To me, who was joined so passionately with the people in this book, it seemed that they were the greatest people I had ever known and the texture of their lives the richest and strangest; and discounting the distortion of judgment that my nearness to them would cause, I think they would seem extraordinary to anyone. If I could get my magnificent people on paper as they were, if I could get down something of their strangeness and richness in my book, I believed that no one would object to my 250,000 words; or, that if my pages swarmed with this rich life few would damn an inept manner and accuse me of not knowing the technique for making a book, as practiced by Balzac, or Flaubert, or Hardy, or Gide. If I have failed to get any of this opulence into my book, the fault lies not in my people – who could make an epic – but in me.

But that is what I wanted to do and tried to do. This book was written in simpleness and nakedness of soul. When I began to write the book twenty months ago I got back something of a child's innocency and wonder. You may question this later when you come to the dirty words. But the dirty words can come out quickly – if the book has any chance of publication, they will come out without conscience or compunction. For the rest, I wrote it innocently and passionately. It has in it much that to me is painful and ugly, but, without sentimentality or dishonesty, it seems to me, because I am a romantic, that pain has an inevitable fruition in beauty. And the book has in it sin and terror and darkness – ugly dry lusts, cruelty, a strong sexual hunger of a child – the dark, the evil, the forbidden. But I believe it has many other things as well, and I wrote it with strong joy, without counting the costs, for I was sure at the time that the whole of my intention – which was to come simply and unsparingly to naked life, and to tell all of my story without affectation or lewdness – would be apparent. At that time I believed it was possible to write of all things, so long as it was honestly done. So far as I know there is not a nasty scene in the book, – but there are the dirty words, and always a casual and unimpeded vision of everything.

When I wrote the book I seized with delight everything that would give it color and richness. All the variety and madness of my people – the leper taint, the cruel waste, the dark flowering evil of life I wrote about with as much exultancy as health, sanity, joy.

It is, of course, obvious that the book is "autobiographical." But, in a literal sense, it is probably no more autobiographical than Gulliver's Travels. There is scarcely a scene that has its base in literal fact. The book is a fiction – it is loaded with invention: story, fantasy, vision. But it is a fiction that is, I believe, more true than fact – a fiction that grew out of a life completely digested in my spirit, a fiction which telescopes, condenses, and objectifies all the random or incompleted gestures of life – which tries to comprehend people, in short, not by telling what people did, but what they should have done. The most literal and autobiographic part of the book, therefore, is its picture of the buried life. The most exact thing in it is its fantasy – its picture of a child's soul.

I have never called this book a novel. To me it is a book such as all men may have in them. It is a book made out of my life, and it represents my vision of life to my twentieth year.

What merit it has I do not know. It sometimes seems to me that it presents a strange and deep picture of American life – one that I have never seen elsewhere; and that I may have some hope of publication. I do not know; I am very close to it. I want to find out about it, and to be told by someone else about it.

I am assured that this book will have a good reading by an intelligent person in a publishing house. I have written all this, not to propitiate you, for I have no peddling instinct, but entreat you, if you spend the many hours necessary for a careful reading, to spend a little more time in giving me an opinion. If it is not a good book, why? If parts are good and parts bad, what are they? If it is not publishable, could it be made so? Out of the great welter of manuscripts that you must read, does this one seem distinguished by any excellence, interest, superior merit?

I need a little honest help. If you are interested enough to finish the book, won't you give it to me?[28]

---

28 / Scribner archives, box 171, folder 1. Wolfe prepared this note to accompany the manuscript of "O Lost," which later became *Look Homeward, Angel.*

Members of the Conference

John D. Baird, *Victoria College, University of Toronto*
G. E. Bentley, Jr., *University College, University of Toronto*
O M Brack, Jr., *University of Iowa*
Wm. R. Cagle, *Indiana University*
Kathleen Coburn, *Victoria College, University of Toronto*
Michael Collie, *York University*
Beatrice Corrigan, *University College, University of Toronto*
Hugh M. Davidson, *Ohio State University*
Joseph Dallett, *Cornell University*
E. J. Devereaux, *University of Western Ontario*
Donald D. Eddy, *Cornell University*
M. S. Elliott, *York University*
David G. Esplin, *University of Toronto Library*
A. G. Falconer, *University College, University of Toronto*
Carlo Fonda, *Algoma College*
Wm. E. Fredeman, *University of British Columbia*
Paul M. Gaudet, *University of Western Ontario*
Phyllis Grosskurth, *University College, University of Toronto*

Francess G. Halpenny, *University of Toronto Press*
Patricia Hernlund, *Wayne State University*
R. P. Hoople, *University of Manitoba*
Wm. J. Howard, *St. Michael's College, University of Toronto*
Glen W. Hunter, *Metropolitan Toronto Central Library*
Jean C. Jamieson, *University of Toronto Press*
M. Jeanneret, *University of Toronto Press*
Beverly Johnston, *McGill University Press*
Weldon A. Kefauver, *Ohio State University Press*
Mrs. Eleanor Kewer, *Harvard University Press*
Basil D. Kingstone, *University of Windsor*
Carl F. Klinck, *University College, University of Western Ontario*
Philip Kolb, *University of Illinois*
Maurice Legris, *University of Alberta*
A. Walton Litz, *Princeton University*
Alec Lucas, *McGill University*
John McClelland, *Victoria College, University of Toronto*
Peter Moes, *Scarborough College, University of Toronto*
Rev. J. P. Morro, *Pontifical Institute of Medieval Studies*
Simon Nowell-Smith, *University of Oxford*
A. C. Nyland, *University of Ottawa*
W. J. B. Owen, *McMaster University*
Sybille Pantazzi, *Art Gallery of Ontario*
George Parker, *Royal Military College*
R. W. Peattie, *University of Calgary*
Barbara Rader, *Yale University Press*
William Ready, *McMaster University*
Themistocles Rodis, *Baldwin-Wallace College*
John M. Robson, *Victoria College, University of Toronto*
Wayland W. Schmitt, *Yale University Press*
R. M. Schoeffel, *University of Toronto Press*
R. J. Schoeck, *St. Michael's College, University of Toronto*
J. A. B. Somerset, *University of Western Ontario*

D. I. B. Smith, *University College, University of Toronto*
Robin Strachan, *McGill University Press*
Thomas E. Tausky, *University of Western Ontario*
Prudence Tracy, *University of Toronto Press*
Dr. and Mrs. D. J. Wurtele, *Carleton University*

Index